To Ella,
With B[...]
from [...]

———— ☆ ————

A
THOUGHT
FOR
EACH DAY
IN
1969

———— ————

THE
FRIENDSHIP
BOOK

OF

FRANCIS GAY

•

1969

D. C. THOMSON & CO. LTD.
LONDON   GLASGOW   MANCHESTER - DUNDEE

Happy the man, and happy he alone,
He who can call today his own —
He who, secure within, can say:
Tomorrow do thy worst, for I have lived today.

JOHN DRYDEN.

HOLIDAYS

We looked with hearts untroubled,
Where skies were always glowing,
And every joy was doubled—
The dreaming, then the going.

DAVID HOPE

SERVICE

The reward that tender service brings,
    The care that does not cease,
Is the trust of tiny, helpless things
    And heart and mind at peace.

DAVID HOPE

JANUARY

GOOD are the things we cannot buy;
*   Eyes that may see a bright blue sky,*
Ears that may catch the voice of spring,
Strength for the tasks each day will bring;
Love and laughter—an appetite,
Sleep that blesses us in the night.

JIMMY GILHOOLEY is over 70 now, but
when this story began, he was a boy of eleven,
and had just started as a miner in Bothwell Colliery.

Unhappily, there was a serious accident at the
pit. Jimmy was trapped under tons of rock, his
legs badly injured. For years, doctors did all they
could for him. But at length Jimmy's mother had to
break the news to him that they could do no more.

That night, on the eve of a new year, Jimmy
made up his mind to give his mother a present
she would never forget. Next morning, when
she went out, he threw back the bedclothes and
lowered his legs to the floor. Gritting his teeth,
and holding on to the furniture, he took one falter-
ing step . . . then another and another. All day he
practised, without a word to a soul.

Then, just as New Year struck, Mrs Gilhooley
heard a step at the kitchen door. She turned—and
there, coming towards her, was her son who she
had thought would never walk again. With tears
of joy, she flung her arms around him.

Now if *you're* hoping for a miracle in this New
Year, remember it will never happen unless, like
Jimmy Gilhooley, you're prepared to do something
about it yourself.

FRIDAY—JANUARY 3.

A LITTLE notice in a newspaper caught my eye. It was inserted by Miss Jane Tosh, a retired school teacher.

It was to all her friends that the notice in the paper was addressed. In it she thanked them for their Christmas and New Year greetings—and then added these words which I will not forget:—

" My hope is that in the New Year they will make the most of the best in life, and the best of the worst."

It has been Miss Tosh's own philosophy all her life, though she'll tell you with a smile that as you grow older it gets more difficult to follow. But surely it is the only way to live—making the most of all the good things life has to offer, and making the best of whatever may bring shadows.

SATURDAY—JANUARY 4.

CHARLIE MAIN is a roadman who, for 20 years, has looked after the hilly, three-and-a-half-mile road between Bo'ness and Linlithgow. No man could have taken more pride in his job. Though, officially, his day wasn't meant to begin until 7 a.m., he was often up at three in the morning to make sure the road was safe for the early traffic.

Every winter's night, when the weather turned frosty, Charlie would go off down the road, just to see how things were. If conditions were bad, you'd find him still on the go at midnight !

Now Charlie has retired, and in appreciation of his years of grand service, he is to be allowed to stay on for as long as he wishes in the roadman's cottage at Borrowstoun.

As I pay tribute to him, I think of all the roadmen like him, who brave blizzard and freezing cold to keep the highways and byways safe.

THE FRIENDSHIP BOOK

SUNDAY—JANUARY 5.

BEHOLD, I stand at the door, and knock.

MONDAY—JANUARY 6.

ELAINE'S father, a widower aged 74, was awarded the M.B.E. He lives happily with Elaine, her husband, and family. The remarkable thing is that this man, who was a civil engineer to trade, having retired and gone to live with his daughter, took up a job as Fire Prevention Officer at a local works, just because he found that he had not enough to do. Now he has become rather an authority on the subject, lectures in different parts of Britain, and sometimes flies abroad on business, too. He is pleased about his M.B.E. ! Isn't it true that a man is just as old as he feels ?

TUESDAY—JANUARY 7.

WHAT will the medical profession do next ?
Have we not all been amazed at the miracles performed by surgeons—giving a new heart to a man. It is a wonderful achievement.

But it is not the first time this has been done, for I have known men and women who have had a complete change of heart, and have gloried in it. They became conscious that their lives fell far short of what they ought to have been, so they fell on their knees in repentance, and they stood up as new men or new women, determined to live more finely.

Our forefathers used to call it conversion. We hear little about it these days, but every day somebody begins again—and in them is a new heart and a new joy. Did not the Psalmist cry: Create in me a clean heart, O God, and renew a right spirit within me ?

WEDNESDAY—JANUARY 8.

I'M not as well-off as I'd like,
Of money I haven't a lot;
The weather is wearing me down,
And cruel afflictions I've got.
But I grin at the thought—" Goodness me,
What a jolly sight worse things could be !"

THURSDAY—JANUARY 9.

NINIAN BROWN is a young man, First Officer on a great merchant ship which regularly plies to the farthest corners of the world.

I have often envied him his travels, thinking of evenings in Naples with smoking Vesuvius in the distance as a backcloth, or of gorgeous butterflies in South America with a wingspan like a bird's . . .

But here is what he said to me recently: " You can go to Tokio or Yokohama, to New York or Rio de Janeiro. The main streets and the centre of the town are all that you are liable to see, and, though the language spoken may be different, they are all very much the same. You will see the same supermarkets, the same fluorescent lighting, much the same goods in the windows, and the same sort of clothes worn by those walking along the pavements."

It is true that all over the world we are tending to see the same films, eat the same foods, drink the same drinks.

So, having thought about it, Francis Gay says to you here: If you like that old hat—wear it. If the jacket is comfortable, why throw it away ? If you dislike the crowd or the pack, then do not be frightened to stay out on your own. Too many things are mass-produced; but there is no need for us to be among them.

THE FRIENDSHIP BOOK

FRIDAY—JANUARY 10.

COLIN FERGUSON is the son of a trawler skipper. In the days of the sailing luggers, his grandfather and great-grandfather were fishermen.

When the time came for Colin to choose his road in life, there was only one thing he wanted to do—go to sea on a trawler—though his mother and father did their best to change his mind, for they knew the hardships and dangers of the life.

Already Colin has come through storms that have threatened to tear out the masts by the roots. He has watched waves that could have swamped the boat towering above the deck. Yet not once has he thought of giving up the life he leads—for the mysterious call of the deep is as strong in him as it was in his forefathers.

Colin and young men like him are our fishermen of the future—I salute them all.

SATURDAY—JANUARY 11.

SHE is 80 years old and one of her sons is abroad, and, oh, how she misses him. But she looks forward more than I can say to the letter he writes every week without fail.

A few weeks ago, however, she couldn't have received a briefer letter:—*Dear Mother, I hope you are well. I am. I'm going to a farm sale today, and have to be very busy. All my love—Jim.*

What a scrappy note. Was it worth the postage?

Oddly enough, I have an idea she thinks as much of this letter as of all the others, no matter how long and newsy they are, for it was written when Jim was rushed off his feet. But he found or made time to send it when he might so easily have neglected to do so. These few lines speak volumes.

All the best, Jim!

SUNDAY—JANUARY 12.

FAITH is the substance of things hoped for, the evidence of things not seen.

MONDAY—JANUARY 13.

THESE lovely lines will echo in every mother's heart—

My days are days of small affairs, of trifling worries, little cares; a lunch to pack, a bed to make, a room to sweep, a pie to bake; a hurt to kiss, a tear to dry, a head to brush, a lace to tie; a face to wash, a toy to mend, a meal to plan, a fuss to end. I, who had hoped some day to gain success, perhaps a bit of fame, must give my life to small affairs, of trifling worries, little cares.

But should tomorrow bring a change, my little house grow still and strange; should all the cares I know today be swept quite suddenly away; where now a hundred duties press, be but an ache of loneliness; no child's gay ribbon to be tied, no wayward little feet to guide—to heaven then would rise my prayers: " Oh, God, give back my little cares."

TUESDAY—JANUARY 14.

ONE of my best friends in the U.S.A. is Sandy MacDougall. Though no man is prouder of being a Scot, Sandy can still enjoy a joke against himself and his countrymen.

In his last letter he told me the story of the old Scotswoman who was sitting up in the candlelight with her dying husband.

" I have to go out now," she said to her man. " So if you feel yourself slipping away, mind and blow out the candle."

WEDNESDAY—JANUARY 15.

SHIVERING on your way to work—
Misery in your feet;
How can you help complaining as
You trudge along the street?
The street's so cold, you'd like instead
A shut-in's warm but weary bed?

THURSDAY—JANUARY 16.

WHAT would you do, my friends, if you were told you would be a semi-invalid, crippled in health, for the rest of your life?

That was the problem that faced a young man of 21, David Thomson. It seemed he had a heart condition for which there was no cure.

Yet, at once, he decided he would not, as the doctors advised, begin to take things easily, in the hope that he might stretch out the time remaining to him. Instead, he would do more than ever, and in the time that was left to him he would try to complete the work of a lifetime.

So he went to university and became a minister. His gifts became so widely known that he was in constant demand as a preacher, and more than once he gave 80 sermons in a week!

Foolish? It might have seemed so, for it could easily have killed him.

Yet in an almost miraculous way, it appeared to give him new strength. The years passed, calls upon him grew greater, and he went on driving himself harder and harder.

Yet today, at over 70, he is still travelling all over the land, preaching and lecturing—for he is none other than the Rev. Dr D. P. Thomson, whose work has been, and still is, such a wonderful influence for good.

THE FRIENDSHIP BOOK

FROM Jimmy Watson's cottage window, you look out over the sea to the far horizon, and below you can see the rocks of the Scaurs of Cruden, a reef on which many vessels have foundered.

There, to warn shipping, is a beacon that flashes night and day—and for 35 years it was Jimmy's task to guard the light, and to report at once to the coastguard if it ever went out.

Time and again, but for him, lives might have been lost. For often it was he who first gave the alarm when a vessel was heading for the rocks in fog.

Now Jimmy's task is over. His last words to his minister were " There must aye be someone to guard the light." You won't find these words in the Bible, but who can doubt that the purpose they enshrine, and the loyalty they reflect are as bright and true as Jimmy's beacon ?

I WAS going to a meeting one evening, and the Lady of the House was finishing the ironing.

Then the iron went dead. Could I help ?

I tinkered around, and in five minutes the " impossible " was accomplished. Everything O K !

It all happened a few weeks ago . . . and then came my electric shock ! Peter, the schoolboy son of a neighbour, dropped in.

He saw my wife ironing, and chuckled. " Still going strong ?" he asked. " If ever the old man makes a mess of it again, just let me know !"

I heard the full story later . . . blown fuse, smell of burning; Lady of the House had rushed round to ask our neighbour to help, and as he was out, young Peter had cleared up the mess I'd made.

Let no man think too highly of himself !

SUNDAY—JANUARY 19.

LET us not be weary in well doing : for in due season we shall reap, if we faint not.

MONDAY—JANUARY 20.

WHEN he was in Troon, Professor William Barclay was approached by a woman who congratulated him on his very successful TV series.

Dr Barclay, a professor at Glasgow University, thanked her sincerely.

The woman went on to say that she would very much like to hear him preach in his own church.

Dr Barclay smiled, " But I don't have a church now," he replied.

" Don't you worry," said the woman sympathetically. " You're bound to get one soon !"

TUESDAY—JANUARY 21.

WHILE we sat chatting with our friend, and looking out through the window, just in a matter of a couple of hours, two men with a yellow bulldozer demolished the walls of a property across the street. Latterly it had been flats, but before that it was probably a small mansion house.

Now, as it tumbled down so quickly, I thought about the people who had been born or lived there; and also about the long months or more it must have taken to build. All the stone would be brought from the quarry by horse and cart. Much of it would be cut by hand-chisel on the spot.

Now new homes will rise in its place. It's progress, and much needed—but I do hope the old way of life won't be forgotten too quickly. There was much to be said for slow, quiet living, and for patience and time spent on craftsmanship.

WEDNESDAY—JANUARY 22.

HER window faces north; her room
Is winter-dark and bare;
Small is her fire; old are her bones—
She's known a load of care.
But folk with troubles like a cup
Of tea with her—she cheers them up!

THURSDAY—JANUARY 23.

A FRIEND remarked the other day that half our troubles are due to lack of self-discipline.

He went on to say that the younger generation has not been taught discipline, and that was the fault of the older generation. He believes that young people get into so much trouble because they have no inward strength to enable them to govern themselves. If they want a thing or are angered they can't control their emotions; they simply must do what they *want* to do.

My friend added with a smile that it wasn't so in his childhood. And earlier than that it was unthinkable. Children *had* to do as they were told. "Why," said he, "Susanna Wesley, mother of John and Charles Wesley, even taught her children to *cry* quietly."

Maybe Mrs Wesley went a little too far, but there is much in what my friend says . . .

FRIDAY—JANUARY 24.

THE other day I came across this saying:—
"Home is the place where we are treated best, yet grumble most."

If that's even a little bit true—and I suspect it is for more than a few of us—then surely it's worth more than a passing thought.

THE FRIENDSHIP BOOK

ALL over the world they talk about Robert Burns. What was it that made him so famous? Was it not that he took the lives and loves of ordinary people, building them up into big themes that would be sung for hundreds of years? He wrote about the people he knew and mixed with. He cared about little places and he wrote about them as if they were great cities. He wrote his very best about them, too.

Other great personalities have emerged from places which were no more important. No one should despise humble origins, either in themselves or in others, for God, too, loved ordinary people.

SUNDAY—JANUARY 26.

LET your speech be alway with grace, seasoned with salt.

MONDAY—JANUARY 27.

IN the village of Kilconquhar, in Fife, many of the houses are all-electric. Very convenient, of course—but what happens if there's a power cut?

That's just what happened on one of the coldest days of the year. And that's where the neighbouring village of Colinsburgh stepped in. Someone commandeered a van. Someone else went round borrowing every spare oil heater they could find. Then it was off to Kilconquhar—and, in no time, every freezing cold house was cosy as pie!

But the good neighbours of Colinsburgh weren't finished yet. They collected flasks and heated up gallons of soup, tea, &c, making sure everyone had something warm to drink.

By the time the power returned the hearts of the Kilconquhar folk were as warm as their homes.

TUESDAY—JANUARY 28.

I WONDER how many have ever heard of Madge Fraser, of Kingussie, who, in her own small way, may also have helped to bring hope to a whole host of folk who will never know her.

Madge has been an invalid for many years. She is in constant pain, and for long spells is unable to leave her bed. All of which might make you think she has troubles enough of her own without worrying about those of other folk.

Not a bit of it! For, from her bed, this brave soul planned and organised a sale of work in the local hall in aid of the British Heart Foundation. She did all the secretarial work, using a tea tray on her knees as a desk. Every day a band of willing neighbours came to her home to get their orders from her. When the great day dawned, everyone was astounded to see that nearly all the beautiful things on the work stall had been sewn by none other than Madge herself!

At the end of the day the great news was brought to Madge that nearly £200 had been raised— and off it went to help doctors and scientists to find the causes and cure of the illness that brings so much tragedy to so many.

As the world acclaims great surgeons and scientists, I acclaim Madge Fraser, who, forgetting herself, remembered others in the finest way.

WEDNESDAY—JANUARY 29.

STRANGE it may seem, yet it is true,
  A sorrow, loss or ill
You might have thought a fatal blow
  Need neither crush nor kill.
With patience, if you do not quit,
It's possible to live with it.

THE FRIENDSHIP BOOK

MRS Patricia Craig is a young Scots mother who emigrated to Australia with her husband. From the very first, they loved Adelaide. They worked hard, saved up, and bought their own house.

Pat has two children now, Ian and June—and the one thing that worried her was the thought that her children wouldn't know what it was to have a grandmother.

Well, Pat decided to advertise for a granny! Believe it or not, she got 18 replies, all from elderly folk who were thrilled at the prospect.

Of course, 18 grannies were too many for one family, so Pat kept five for herself and matched up the other 13 with lonely immigrants who also yearned for a granny for their children. Now she visits the five with the children and welcomes them to her home. And, to Ian and June, there's simply no one like them.

For me at any rate, it's a story like this that makes up for much in the news that's so depressing.

I FOUND these words on a calendar—
" The years teach more than the years ever know."

But do they? Surely, what we learn day by day is mostly forgotten, because it has to do with trifles.

But as the years go by the over-all pattern emerges. The truth dawns upon us that happenings have consequences. We think we can cheat, and so we can, and get away with it. But, looking back, we see that in fact, we have been cheating ourselves, and that our gains are offset by greater losses in character.

The years do indeed teach us more than all the days taken one by one. Happy is the man or woman whose increasing years bring no regrets.

FEBRUARY

A GREAT storm of wind and rain. Branches torn from the trees lying all over the road. A felt hat lying abandoned among the traffic. Down from the top of the building where workmen were trying to secure a chimney came another cap, to be retrieved by a lady in the street.

Isn't it odd that man, who is even now able to think of sending people to the moon, still hasn't been able to invent an everyday item like a hat that will remain secure in the strongest gale?

IF God be for us, who can be against us?

AT the dentist's the other morning, and I am happy to report that the interview could have been much more painful! Afterwards we looked at his engagement book to arrange my next appointment.

" Will you look at these two names squeezed in here, Mr Gay ?" he asked, pointing with his finger at the open page. " Both of them insisting on seeing me at once, though I know it is not urgent in either case. Now here, further over, is a name that really matters, and he says, ' Just take me when you can. I'll arrange my other appointments to suit '."

That's life, isn't it ? Here are one or two of no great consequence, expecting all kinds of privileges. Here is someone else, whose days are busy and whose time is vital, saying—" Just fit me in when you can."

TUESDAY—FEBRUARY 4.

THIS story really began over 100 years ago, when a Thurso lad of eleven called Willie Smith started his own army!

I don't suppose that any of Willie's fearless " soldiers " was more than 13 years old, yet in a way, that trusty little band was destined to become an untold influence for good.

For when he grew up, Willie went to work with his uncle in Glasgow. There it grieved him to see how the lives of many boys were wasted. Indeed, every time he passed a street corner, he felt stirred to do something for the boys he saw there—and at length he believed he had found the answer.

So, one evening in 1883, Willie and two friends who helped him in the children's mission met and knelt to ask a blessing on the new organisation for boys that Willie had planned. None of them dreamed it would one day reach out to every corner of the world—but it did, for it became the Boys' Brigade, the movement that has helped to shape the lives and characters of countless boys.

When Willie died, he was Sir William Smith, honoured by king and country and a multitude of grateful men and boys. It's more than 85 years since the B.B. was founded, yet who can doubt that the spirit that inspired that little band so long ago is marching still, steadfast as ever.

WEDNESDAY—FEBRUARY 5.

IF in winter you choose to be glum,
It's easy as easy can be;
But just moaning and groaning all day
Seems useless and silly to me.
If the sun doesn't shine in the sky,
Wear a smile — or at any rate TRY!

THURSDAY—FEBRUARY 6.

WE had thought that our new friend, Gordon, was a bachelor, but it turned out when we reached this artist's house that several children were running through the place. Could we have been so wrong?

They proved to be the children from next door, who had recently lost their mother. At the moment their father was out working, and here was Gordon, their neighbour, not only giving them the run of his house, but also cooking their lunch. " Keep on practising !" he shouted from the kitchen, where he had just opened the oven door. I learned that he was also teaching one of the boys to play the flute.

A heart of charity, it seems, can be found not in mothers only.

FRIDAY—FEBRUARY 7.

NELLIE has had years of illness and suffering, and is no stranger to hospital wards and operating theatres. But she tells me she has a stand-by that never fails her, and which I believe may help many of you, too.

It is simply this. Every time Nellie starts the journey from the ward to the operating theatre she quietly begins to repeat the words of the 23rd Psalm. If she says them very slowly she finds they last the whole way—along the busy corridors, down in the lift, and past the wards, ending just as she reaches the doors that lead into the theatre.

Nellie adds simply, " I'm no braver than anyone else, but the strange thing is that I've never known fear inside these doors . . ."

Strange ? Perhaps not, for can you think of any prayer more uplifting for those who go forward, like Nellie, to face the unknown?

THE WAY OF THE GEESE

Where are they come from?
Where do they go?
Where will they be tomorrow?
The greylags go their airy ways
And I would that I could follow.

DAVID HOPE

THE UNSEEN GIFT

Our spires were built by men who strove
In humble stone and lime,
And glorified the daily task
With faith that conquers time.

DAVID HOPE

SATURDAY—FEBRUARY 8.

" IT is possible to find cities without walls, without kings, without wealth, without letters, without theatres, but a city without a temple or that practiseth not worship, no man ever saw." Plutarch wrote this long ago.

And according to Emmanuel Kant there are three beliefs essential if life is to have real meaning. These three are—(a) belief in God, (b) belief in freedom, (c) belief in immortality. The most important of the three, he says, is belief in God.

SUNDAY—FEBRUARY 9.

LORD, Thou knowest all things; Thou knowest that I love Thee.

MONDAY—FEBRUARY 10.

THE lady stood silently beside us on the seafront at Fraserburgh. There was little wind, but the ground swell was sending enormous waves over the breakwater. The harbour was closed to shipping. " My husband sent me down to see the storm," she told us presently, " because he said it was so like the day when the lifeboat was lost with all hands in February 1953." She went on to describe that tragedy just as if it had happened yesterday.

" You remember all about it," said the Lady of the House.

" Yes," said the stranger, " you see, it was only two days after it took place that I was married. It's still most vivid to me."

I never cease to wonder at the way in which joy and sorrow are mixed together so closely in life. But, of course, this is what gives life its savour and makes it worth the living.

TUESDAY—FEBRUARY 11.

MAY I tell you the parable of the bus driver?
The bus driver's name is Ron Dewhurst, and
for ten years he spent his working day driving a long-
distance coach. He enjoyed his work. He liked seeing
new places and new faces. I don't suppose he ever
expected he'd do any other job.

Then one day he heard Rev. Tom Allan preaching. Something in the minister's message stirred
Ron—and later, listening to Dr Billy Graham, he
knew he must leave his job and become a missionary.

Oh, it seemed ridiculous—a bus driver wanting
to be a missionary. After all, all he'd known for ten
years was bus driving, and what good was that to
a missionary? But, trusting where he could not
see, he began to train for the mission-field. And
would you believe it? He found that a mission in
South America was desperately needing a man with
bus-driving experience to take charge of their Bible
Coach—a bus that goes all over the Argentine,
carrying Bibles and Testaments to villages far
from civilisation.

So now Ron and his wife spend eleven months of
the year in the Bible Coach, covering thousands of
miles among primitive folk, telling them of the faith
on which they staked their lives.

There can be no prouder tribute to Ron than
to say he is still a bus driver to the glory of God.

WEDNESDAY—FEBRUARY 12.

WHEN children shout and run about
Like leaping flames of fire,
When they can eat and eat and eat,
And never seem to tire;
Don't wish they'd quietly sit still—
They do that only if they're ill!

THURSDAY—FEBRUARY 13.

A FRIEND was visiting a retired minister. On the mantelpiece sat a tiny mouse carved from an acorn. The minister told my friend it had belonged to one of the finest women he had ever known.

She was a nurse in Edinburgh Royal Infirmary, and her name was Betty Garrow. But no one ever called her that, for she was known far and wide as " Sister Sunshine." Why, even on the dullest day she seemed to carry sunshine with her wherever she went. Even when she herself was incurably ill, the old smile was still there.

And though it is more than ten years since she died, she is remembered in a unique way. Every week a fresh posy of flowers is placed in the ward where she worked, in her memory. It is put there, I'm told, by someone whose name will never be known, but who owes her a debt he can never repay.

So, in a way, Sister Sunshine is still spreading joy in the place where she did so much for so many.

FRIDAY—FEBRUARY 14.

ONE of my friends runs a school of motoring. He has been sharing with me one or two incidents which are worth passing on.

One is of the very " with it " girl who was one of his pupils, and asked him, while she was driving, if he ever went to a Saturday evening dance. " No, not now," my friend replied. " I expect I've become a square."

The young lady treated him to a smile. " Oh," said she, " I wouldn't say that. But if you are a square you have nicely rounded corners !"

SATURDAY—FEBRUARY 15.

I READ recently the old tale of a young woman who visited a fortune-teller.

The Wise One said—" You'll be poor and unmarried till you are forty."

Eagerly her client inquired—" And what then ?"

" Then," said the fortune-teller, " you'll get used to it !"

Cold comfort, indeed. But there is some truth in it. The fact is, there's an art in accepting what cannot be changed, in living with the troubles of the times, and by this very act making them tell as little as possible on you.

SUNDAY—FEBRUARY 16.

IN Him we live, and move, and have our being.

MONDAY—FEBRUARY 17.

MRS MACDONALD was telling me how she has just succeeded in reuniting a little boy called Colin with his mother and stepfather. A voluntary welfare worker, she warns—" Don't think that all my cases are such a success, but one such success makes up for many disappointments."
She went on to describe how, when Colin's mother was married for the second time, the new husband would not accept the child, and so they were parted. Now Colin is at last happy again. " Indeed," Mrs Macdonald added, " they are all so very happy. The little boy's face, which was pale and withdrawn, lights up every time I go to visit that place."

Of herself she added as an afterthought, " I love my church and I love going there; but it is so important to do something practical, to have a practical as well as a church-going religion."

TUESDAY—FEBRUARY 18.

HENRY BAKER was born in London about 150 years ago, the son of an Admiral.

When he inherited his father's title and estate, Henry could have lived a life of ease and plenty as a country squire. But instead he preferred to work as a parson in a little parish amid the orchards of Herefordshire, ministering faithfully to his flock, content to be their helper and friend.

It was there that he wrote six verses of a hymn that has become beloved the world over—" The King Of Love My Shepherd Is." Though he wrote many more hymns, I believe that was the one Henry himself prized most dearly—and as he lay dying, the last words he ever spoke were a verse from it—

> Perverse and foolish oft I strayed,
> But yet in love He sought me;
> And on His shoulder gently laid,
> And home rejoicing brought me.

He knew that, though he had striven to live a good life, he had often fallen short, just as all of us have. And it was a source of infinite joy and wonder to him to know that, no matter how far he had strayed from the path, his Maker followed him and led him back again.

It is a glorious affirmation of a great promise which is as true for us today as it was for him.

WEDNESDAY—FEBRUARY 19.

> I'M telling you it's odd, but true,
>   The richest folk are not
> The ones who simply are not wise
>   To how much wealth they've got.
> The rich are kindly folk who smile
> And warm our hearts a little while.

THE FRIENDSHIP BOOK

IT was such a little thing, really—merely a book. She bought it, took it home, gave it to her schoolboy son. He was pleased to receive the gift, and read and read.

That was nice for Mum—she got a bit of peace.

The book was about astronomy. When Patrick began to read it, he knew no more about stars than any bright boy. When he had finished, his mind and heart were conquered. He determined there and then to be an astronomer, and an astronomer he became—Patrick Moore, whose B.B.C. talks in recent years have fascinated millions.

All because of a mother's little gift.

Who would have thought it?

WHILE tidying up the living-room, the Lady of the House paused with a shabby and faded book in her hands. " Francis," she said, " I've never seen you read this in all the years we've been married—and it really doesn't look very attractive. May I throw it out?"

I stroked my chin. " Well," I said gently, " you may—but, if you don't mind, I'd rather like to keep it. Let's put it in the box-room."

I was opening it as I spoke. Then I showed the fly-leaf to my wife. " A very old friend of mine wrote these words in it the day he gave it me long ago," I said. " It sounds old-fashioned these days—but it's true."

Then the Lady of the House read:—When you have nothing left but God, you become aware for the first time that God is enough.

My wife made no comment. She merely patted the old book, and put it back among the rest.

SATURDAY—FEBRUARY 22.

I MAKE no bones about borrowing this little thought from the Scottish Y.M.C.A. " Bulletin," where I read recently that any church congregation consists of four kinds of bones—

WISHBONES—members who want somebody else to do the work.

JAWBONES—members who talk a lot but do very little else.

KNUCKLEBONES — members who knock everything others try to do.

BACKBONES—members who roll up their sleeves and get on with the work.

SUNDAY—FEBRUARY 23.

CHARITY suffereth long, and is kind.

MONDAY—FEBRUARY 24.

THESE lines were found in an old book:—

So long as there are homes to which men turn at close of day,
So long as there are homes where children are and women stay;
If love and loyalty and faith be found across those sills,
A stricken nation can recover from its greatest ills.
So long as there are homes where fires burn and there is bread,
So long as there are homes where lamps are lit and prayers said;
Although a people falter through the dark, and nations grope,
If God Himself is in those little homes, we must have hope.

THE FRIENDSHIP BOOK

ONE Wednesday a song-thrush somehow found
its way down the pit shaft at Overton Colliery,
Wishaw, and deep into the heart of the mine. As
the day-shift ended they told the men on night-shift
to keep a look-out for the bird—for the colliery was
to close down at the week-end.

The night-shift saw the bird—but, try as they
might, they couldn't capture it. All day on Thursday,
as they worked, the miners kept watch for the
thrush, but still it eluded them. On Friday it was
still there, and as the last shift went down the mine
they declared they wouldn't return until they had
found the bird and brought it to safety.

So, when the shift ended, the miners took their
lamps and searched silently through the deserted
galleries of the pit, one after the other, until at
last, high in a crevice, they came upon the thrush.

Gently one of the miners reached up and grasped
the frightened bird in his hand. Then, placing it
in his helmet, he and the others made their way to
the shaft, and so to the open air again. There the
miner lifted the thrush out of his helmet and opened
his hand. For a moment the bird sat motionless—
—then soared into the sky.

It's a wonderful thing, isn't it, that a band of
miners should be so concerned about the life of one
tiny bird, and how happy I am to tell you of it.

WEDNESDAY—FEBRUARY 26.

WHEN days are dark and nights are long,
    There's very little fun
In being old and all alone—
    Your busy life now done.
But when a friend knocks at the door
There's room in life for you once more.

A DAY TO REMEMBER

In youth it's good to test your strength,
To lead and keep the pace,
The joy of striving then is yours,
And life's a well-run race;
In later years you'll smile and say,
" Was that really me that day?"

DAVID HOPE

POTATO TIME

Your hands are cold,
The gaffers scold,
The day seems never-ending.
But a joke and song
Help time along —
Then homeward we are wending.

And then for tea—
Ah, spuds I see,
Chipped or mashed or boiling.
No other food
Tastes half so good
As that we get by toiling.

DAVID HOPE

BEHIND THE DREAM

It's fun to plan a garden
In beauty all arrayed,
But lovely dreams will not come true
Without the fork and spade.

DAVID HOPE

THE FRIENDSHIP BOOK

ALTHOUGH these are ten-second sermons, each one on its own is worth a lot of thought—

When success turns your head, you're facing failure.

Sympathy is two hearts pulling at one load.

Worry gives little things big shadows.

Anger is only one letter short of danger.

Life's difficulties and disappointments are meant to make us better, not bitter.

It is unending sunshine that turns good soil into a desert.

The man who falls down usually gets up quicker than the man who lies down.

Life's greatest tragedy is to lose God and not miss Him.

WALKING along the street, the Lady of the House was rather terrified by three young hooligans who were going along the pavement before her. They were shouting and bawling, or swinging from a scaffolding which projected from a building. Other pedestrians were keeping carefully out of their way.

Then their way was blocked by an old man hesitating at the roadside; so frail that he was scarcely fit to be out. Would they push him into the gutter where the cars and buses were rushing past? Not a bit of it! Surrounding him, they took him by the arm, led him carefully across the street, and put him carefully on to the bus he wanted.

It is so easy to judge or even to condemn others by their superficial appearance. Here were these three, apparently no more than ruffians, but still with their hearts in the right place.

MARCH

TO those in need of help, those weighed down by worries and cares, and those who feel they are at the end of their tether, I pass on these sixteen words, sent to me by a friend who has found them to be true —

When you dig another out of his troubles, you find a place to bury your own.

THE Lord is my light.

THE three young people came into the sweetie shop where George Carmichael and I stood just passing the time of day. The biggest of the three lifted his nose until it was nearly level with the counter. " Anything for a penny, please?" he asked politely. Indeed George had!

He walked solemnly from behind the counter and pushed forward towards the children a three-tiered tea-trolley, loaded with little things. " Everything on the bottom shelf is 3d," he explained, " the middle shelf is 2d, and everything on the top shelf is 1d." We stood watching these shy customers as slowly and carefully they made their choices.

George spent a good ten minutes with the children and the money involved was practically nothing. Yet I think he made a lot of profit. He gained much through the confidence of these little ones in himself, and the fact that they knew they could come to him and not be bullied and rushed out of his way. I'm glad I know George.

TUESDAY—MARCH 4.

IF you ever stepped into Harry Gill's office and looked at his desk, you would have seen all the signs of a busy man—telephone, files, ledgers and piles of correspondence.

Yet, despite all the pressure and responsibility of his job, he was never known to lose his patience or his temper—and his secret was to be found in something else that lay on his desk. It was a Bible. Often during the day, when things were difficult, Harry would turn up one of his favourite passages, and when he had read it, everything somehow seemed so much easier to cope with.

Not many knew, either, that for years he had visited an old, blind man in a home. Harry had heard the old man was all alone and, busy as he was, he made it his business to go and see him often.

There is so much more I could tell you about Harry, but now his mission is over, for he died suddenly at only 50. At his funeral service, how right it seemed that the last hymn should not be one of sadness, but of triumph—" Soldiers of Christ, Arise !" I cannot think of a finer epitaph:—

> That, having all things done,
> And all your conflicts passed,
> Ye may o'ercome through Christ alone,
> And stand complete at last.

WEDNESDAY—MARCH 5.

> *Y OU'VE tried and failed, and tried again ?*
> *For you there is no sun ?*
> *Your strength is gone, you CAN'T keep on ?*
> *Life's pilgrimage is done ?*
> *So you may think, but press on still —*
> *There's light beyond the rain-lashed hill !*

THURSDAY—MARCH 6.

SOME time ago I was shown round a school. I met the headmaster, the staff and pupils.

But what I remember most was five minutes I spent with the school caretaker!

Middle-aged, limping, but keen-eyed, lively and overflowing with pride in his cloakrooms and classrooms and corridors, his windows and ceilings, proud to show them because they were all clean as a new pin and kept in trim condition.

" The children here mean a lot to me," he told me. " I'm proud to be able to keep the place neat and tidy. I feel that if I do my job as it was meant to be done—or a bit better — then I can go to bed feeling I've done a good job well. It makes me very happy to know that the headmaster attends to his business and I attend to mine . . . and between us we keep this school up to scratch!"

I shook hands with that caretaker . . . a proud and happy man.

FRIDAY—MARCH 7.

THEY were paying an annual five shillings—a nominal rent for the use of a former school as a place of worship. A fine building in its day, slowly through the years it was becoming more and more neglected. Then word came from the architects: " You must get out at once. The whole fabric is in a dangerous condition." The congregation is now faced with the urgent problem of finding a new place, or raising a lot of money.

Of course, they should have been putting a little by each year. It's no bad idea in the moral sphere as well to store up small achievements, happy memories and good friends against the days when they may be needed.

THE FRIENDSHIP BOOK

"SHOULD a housewife work a five-day week, the same as the men?" This is what someone asked. If any government or trade union passed such legislation, no woman worth the name would pay the slightest attention. If a child in the home were ill, she would attend to it, if need be, throughout the twenty-four hours and seven days of the week. Nor would she let a girl or boy go off to school with a torn tunic or blazer, just because it happened to be her day off! Here we see love, gentleness and patience; surely acting in the place of God, with patient understanding.

THERE is a friend that sticketh closer than a brother.

I DON'T wish to be dubbed a false prophet and I am very anxious not to be classed as an over-cheerful optimist. What I am venturing to say now, I say with due caution and proper restraint, but I am compelled to say it. Only this very morning I was roused by the chirping of birds; and only a morning or two ago I found indications of colour about to break out of the brave green crocuses in the garden and the promise of green leaves one day where the sycamore buds were showing signs of hidden life.

Far be it from me to lead anyone astray or to prompt unjustifiable hopes, but I must say that however cold the day or whatever storms may come, I have an idea that eventually winter will give place to spring!

TUESDAY—MARCH 11.

A FRIEND of mine was visiting Paisley and, after midnight, as he walked through the town to his hotel, he was the only figure on the street apart from the policeman on the beat. But as he approached Paisley Abbey, he was puzzled to see the great windows ablaze with light. Who could be there, he wondered, at this late hour?

Suddenly he was given the answer. For, from the Abbey came the glorious music of the choir and organ—and, soaring above them, a voice that could belong to only one man. It was Kenneth McKellar singing " The Lord's My Shepherd."

It seems that, for a long time, Kenneth had wanted to make a recording of the best-loved psalms and hymns of Scots folk—and he wanted to make it in the town where he was born, and in the Abbey where, as a boy, he used to sing. But there was one snag—the Abbey stands on a busy main road, and the noise of passing traffic would spoil the record. So it was decided to make the recording in the small hours of the morning, when the streets were silent.

That is why, as my friend walked through the darkness in Paisley he was rewarded with that thrilling moment.

When at last he moved on, he took with him a memory that will, he says, live with him for the rest of his days.

WEDNESDAY—MARCH 12.

A LITTLE bit of sunshine is magical, indeed,
　　It fills the world with colour,
It wakes the sleeping seed.
A little bit of sunshine from any kindly face
Can make this dreary planet
A very happy place!

THURSDAY—MARCH 13.

WE sat, eight or nine of us, holding a committee meeting of those who were organising the flag day and certain other things. We met in the comfortable front room of the secretary's house. "The fire's getting low," said Ella, "will you please fill up the scuttle, Vernon?" Her husband rose like a lamb.

When coffee was brought in, after our business was past, Vernon was called upon once more to do his stuff. Nor would Ella accept the help of the two or three ladies who were present.

Now there is no kinder wife in all the world than Ella, and no better mother. But she should consider well before she gives such orders to her husband in front of others. A man has his pride. Come to think of it, no more should men take their wives for granted, rapping out orders in public. Observers hear only what is said, catching nothing of the underlying love, and they can jump too easily to the wrong conclusions.

FRIDAY—MARCH 14.

THIS is an extract from a letter from a friend in Australia—

"I would love to come back to the old country and see you all again, but to make the trip worthwhile I would need a month's holiday at the very least. But my boss will never let me go for so long a time at a stretch, although I can have as many short holidays as I want. He is going to Europe himself this summer, so maybe he'll change his point of view when he comes back——"

Isn't it curious how once we have undergone a particular experience we are far better able to see the other person's point of view?

SATURDAY—MARCH 15.

I FOUND this story in "The Thunder of Bare Feet," by J. Wallace Hamilton —

A sheepman in Indiana was troubled by dogs which were killing his sheep. Sheepmen usually counter that problem by law suits, barbed wire fences or even shotguns, but this man went to work with a better idea. To every neighbour's child he gave a lamb or two as pets.

In due time his neighbours had their own small flocks. Families with dogs began to tie them up, or train them. Soon the problem was solved!

This brings to mind the words of St Paul: Be not overcome of evil, but overcome evil with good.

SUNDAY—MARCH 16.

GOD shall wipe away all tears from their eyes.

MONDAY—MARCH 17.

BILL ARCHIBALD looks after a community centre. Of course, he meets a lot of friendly folk there, and one day he heard about an old lady who lived alone and found her life terribly lonely.

Bill thought maybe she'd like a budgie to keep her company. So he took one along to her — and what a pleasure it was to see the way her face lit up.

Indeed, Bill was so moved that he decided to give away more budgies to lonely old folk—and believe it or not, in five years he gave away no fewer than 600. Every one has found its way into the home of some old person, where its cheeky chirp and bright eyes have meant more than words can ever say.

Bill is doing a wonderful job in bringing the blessing of a budgie to so many lonely homes.

ANYTHING FOR ME?

If postie gives your house a miss
The reason's often simply this —
We'd like to keep our friendships bright
But find it such a bore to write.

DAVID HOPE

TIME

The hour-glass tells us time is flying,
  Make the most of every minute.
But try, before the day is dying,
  To put some act of friendship in it.

DAVID HOPE

TUESDAY—MARCH 18.

ONE of the most amazing happenings in the realm of nature is the punctual migrations of the swallows which raise their young about the famous monastery of San Juan Capistrano, in California.

Shortly before dawn on the morning of October 23, the tens of thousands of swallows associated with the mission, fly south with a whirring of wings; and for some eighty years the birds have returned on the 19th of March, appearing as a tiny grey cloud on the horizon, and shaping their course across the Pacific with unerring accuracy.

How is it that the swallows arrive and depart on time ? How do they know the time to within a few hours ? Why are they never late or early ? What inward " clock " speeds them on their way, and by what knowledge, unknown to us, do they find their way across trackless miles ?

I mention this because springtime is with us again, and the world about us is breaking into fresh beauty. There must be something wrong with us if we can see this miracle of rebirth without wondering, questioning. Life itself is far more amazing than most of us realise, infinitely more mysterious. To the mission of San Juan Capistrano return the swallows on the 19th of March every year.

How ?

WEDNESDAY—MARCH 19.

I SAID " It's cold."
The farmer's smile
Showed I was little knowing.
" I've wanted this
For quite a while,
It's just the day for sowing."

THURSDAY—MARCH 20.

ON my desk is a letter from a broken and despairing man.

He is enduring loneliness and remorse. He has brought suffering on himself and others. He has lost almost everything that is worth anything.

He says in his letter, " It's no use praying—God could never forgive me."

Well, to this man I have said this—

Faith knows nothing of mathematics. However silly it may sound it is, in a sense, true that the further you are from God, the nearer God is to you. The worse you are, in a sense, the more God loves you. That is not to say God is far from a good man or that he loves a good man less than a bad. It simply means that the greater your need, the more you can be helped and sustained; the lower you have fallen, the higher you can be lifted.

If, in your distress, you pray sincerely to be forgiven, and for your life to be reshaped so that in time you can make amends, God will work a miracle in you, raise you up, give you a new vision and new strength, and create a new man in you.

FRIDAY—MARCH 21.

THE Lady of the House picked up this gem in a big store.

Two folk were chatting at one of the stalls, and the first asked, " Have you seen Mrs Ramsay lately ?"

" Oh, yes," was the reply. " She came round yesterday morning, and stayed over an hour."

" Ah," commented the first lady, " so you'll know all there is to know !"

" Not I," retorted Mrs Ramsay's neighbour. " That woman can talk all day without saying anything !"

SATURDAY—MARCH 22.

THE meter reader, having left his van, arrived at the cottage in the glen, away at the end of a rough track. Having read the meter carefully, he exclaimed. " Only three or four units again! Do you never use electricity?" " I do that," said the old man, who lived alone. " It's lit every night to find the matches before I light the lamps and it helps me to go to bed after I put them out."

For that old man the knowledge that the electric power was there when he needed it was enough. It helped him keep his own lamps burning.

And surely this is like God's loving help—there for us all when we need it, and ever helping us to keep our own lamps burning.

SUNDAY—MARCH 23.

SEEK ye the Lord while He may be found.

MONDAY—MARCH 24.

MUST share one tiny bit of good news.

Not exactly world-shattering news, but I am glad about it even though the action takes place rather early and scarcely under the most favourable conditions. I am told, however, that I shall benefit from the results before very long.

The news is that the Lady of the House has begun spring cleaning. Not on a big scale as yet—but certain drawers and cupboards have been seen to. The box-room has been turned out, everything dusted and almost everything put back.

You may wonder why I am so pleased that the spring cleaning has begun. Well, my reason is rather obvious, I imagine. Whether I like it or not: the sooner it is begun, the sooner it will be finished !

TUESDAY—MARCH 25.

IF you'd happened to pop in to the eventide home you would have got the surprise of your life.

You'd have found yourself in the middle of a gay Easter parade, with all the old ladies sporting their brightest bonnets. You see, the matron had announced a special competition for the bonniest Easter bonnet—and, my goodness, what an air of secrecy there was that morning.

Many of the old ladies shut themselves up in their bedrooms while they fashioned their bonnets. Others toddled away on mysterious errands, and when no one was looking, sped back to their rooms again. You've no idea of the goings-on there were !

Then when the tea-time bell sounded, they all sallied forth—and what a show of Easter bonnets. Some were decked with daffodils and tulips. Some were swathed in coloured paper. Others were trimmed with outsize bows. One old body even had a big bunch of black grapes pinned to her hat.

You can guess what a time the judges had trying to decide where the three prizes should go. But, eventually, they chose the winners, and the prizes were handed out while everybody clapped and cheered.

All of which surely goes to show that those who imagine eventide homes are sad and serious places couldn't be more wrong if they tried !

WEDNESDAY—MARCH 26.

SHE loved the light, her eyes were bright,
*   She died not long ago;*
We missed her smile and mourned awhile,
*   Our grief, how CAN you know ?*
But dare we always sigh and weep
For one who laughed, then fell asleep ?

THE FRIENDSHIP BOOK

HER Majesty's Inspector was asking the class the name of the poet who wrote "To a Skylark": "Bird of the wilderness blithesome and cumberless . . ." The young teacher, unseen to the inspector, was stabbing her finger in the direction of one of the pupils. At last one of the others grasped her meaning. "Please, sir, it was James Hogg, the Ettrick Shepherd." The teacher heaved a sigh of relief. But even had the inspector noticed her gesture, it is unlikely that he would have guessed that that boy's name, too, was James Hogg! No marks for honesty, but full marks to the teacher for quick thinking!

FRIDAY—MARCH 28.

ONE night a young man sat with a friend who was dying. As the slow, dark hours ticked away, the two spoke quietly of the things of eternity. Somehow, in that hushed room, the young man found new meaning to his faith, and a few years later he became minister of a little Devon village. He took his friend's orphaned children with him.

He laboured there until the end of his days, and before he died, he said his great wish was that some words of his might live on after he had gone, to comfort the broken-hearted and inspire those whose faith was flagging.

He was never to know how richly his dream would come true—for his name was Henry Francis Lyte, who gave us two of the greatest hymns ever written, "Abide With Me" and "Praise, My Soul, The King of Heaven." Suffering as he himself was, he could still find it in his heart to write: —

> Ransomed, healed, restored, forgiven—
> Who like me His praise should sing?

SATURDAY—MARCH 29.

LAST summer, four friends set out from Aberdeen for a picnic.

They took the road to Strathdon, and when they stopped they found themselves gazing at the little church of Glenbuchat, which has stood for nearly 500 years. It was a perfect spot, and one of the four, a minister, thought what an inspiring place it would be for a service. For, though the church has been beautifully restored and is kept bright and clean, it is no longer used.

Well, the outcome was that there was a service there. For the minister returned to Glenbuchat, and with him he brought his choir from Aberdeen. It was a lovely afternoon, and the little kirk nestling amid the high hills had never looked better.

When the visitors arrived, the bell was rung for the first time for 27 years, and folk came from miles around and gathered in the kirk.

When the service ended and the congregation streamed out, all who were there felt they had shared in something they would always remember.

Oh, yes, stained-glass windows and fine organs are all very well—but I often think it is in simplicity that we come nearest to the heart of our faith.

SUNDAY—MARCH 30.

SURELY He hath borne our griefs, and carried our sorrows.

MONDAY—MARCH 31.

I LIKE schoolboy howlers. Here is one I came across the other day.

"Abraham Lincoln was born in a log hut in Kentucky which he built with his own hands."

APRIL

TUESDAY—APRIL 1.

A RING at the door and in walked a tall, hand-some, young man with a bunch of flowers for the Lady of the House.

I kept an eye on him, as you may well believe. Especially as I had never seen him before, and he even had the impudence to make it plain he was not interested in me, but in my wife.

Anyhow, I took him into the living-room, and he handed over the bouquet with a smile and asked if she remembered him. " Vaguely," confessed the Lady of the House, " but I just can't recall your name." (I was glad about that, anyhow.)

" You don't remember Arthur?"

Well, Arthur is not exactly Britain's rarest masculine name, and my wife still looked puzzled, though evidently enjoying the presence of a prosperous-looking and polite visitor. " Arthur?" she repeated.

He chuckled. " I should be a schoolboy of about fourteen," he explained. " I am now twenty-eight . . . it makes a bit of difference. I'm living and working in London, but I've been up to see my old Granny, and she says you keep looking in to have a crack with her. So, if you don't mind, I've just come to say thank you."

WEDNESDAY—APRIL 2.

*A*S *with a trumpet shrill, again*
 The Easter world awakes;
Drab soil grows green, new life is seen,
 What music each bird makes !
Though you have failed, sing this refrain:
I can, I will begin again !

THURSDAY—APRIL 3.

WHEN a teacher arrived at a school in the English Midlands a few weeks ago, she took over a class of backward seven-year-olds, including Brian.

Brian was disconsolate. At home, for a year, he had been blamed for laziness. There was apparently proof of this because he was making no progress whatever in his sums. At school his teacher kept calling him to her desk, showing him his arithmetic book—nine sums marked with a cross because they were wrong. Teacher said that he was a blockhead.

Then came the young teacher. She took a look at Brian, and another at Brian's hopeless arithmetic book. Every time she marked the latter she omitted to put crosses by the sums which were wrong. *But she put a tick by every sum that was right.*

And I hear that already Brian is coming on fine.

FRIDAY—APRIL 4.

A DRAPER'S list published in 1797 gives the following scale of charges:—Cloak—4s 6d. Shoes—3s 9d. Stockings—1s 6d. Plain dress—6s 6d. Petticoat—4s 6d.

It is hard, nevertheless, to say how much any particular sum of money was worth in the past. The real question is—how long does it take to earn the money to pay your rent? Or to buy certain clothes?

Once upon a time there was a man who betrayed his Master for thirty pieces of silver. What he could have bought with it is uncertain, but what he lost we know for sure. He lost his soul. The justice which condemned him still rules this world. There is nothing that anyone can earn, no cash prize anyone can win, no shining new car or splendid home that is worth touching if it is given in exchange for a reputation—or a soul.

THE FRIENDSHIP BOOK

WHAT a host of different creeds there are, and how the theologians argue one with the other! It has been so for centuries, and seems no nearer an end. Some say religion is this, others that, and while the erudite discuss details, the world is hungry for bread and for guidance in right living day by day.

And yet even before Christ came, Micah said simply and straightforwardly—*What doth the Lord require of thee, but to do justly and to love mercy, and to walk humbly with thy God?*

I KNOW that my redeemer liveth, and that He shall stand at the latter day upon the earth.

SHE isn't poor. She isn't ill. She isn't old and stiff. And she's neither deaf nor blind. But, poor soul, her husband left her years ago, and not one of her three children ever sleeps a night in her house, though all pay her short visits now and then.

This woman, whom I pity, has never told a lie or stolen anything, as far as I know. She is, in fact, a regular church attender. But there's one peculiar fault in her which has ruined her life—and made life tragic for others.

She's unlivable with. That's all there is to it. She belongs to the awkward squad. No matter how anyone tries to be kind to her, she rubs them up the wrong way, says bitter things, interprets everything in a way never intended, and so on . . .

As I say, I'm sorry for her. She could have been happy all along, but she stands in her own light.

THE FRIENDSHIP BOOK

TUESDAY—APRIL 8.

THIS story begins in Stirling, where Janet
McGorty has her home. Janet went through
a serious operation, but, home again, she appeared
well on the road to recovery.

Then, at one o'clock one morning, Janet's sister,
Morna, suddenly heard her cry out. When Morna
switched on the light, she found Janet dangerously
ill and struggling for breath. Morna ran to a neighbour and asked her to phone for an ambulance.
Then she hurried back to Janet's side, desperately
afraid it would be too late.

But it wasn't—for, so quickly that she could
hardly believe it, the ambulance pulled up at the
door. Kindly, but firmly, the two ambulance men
took command. They carried a portable oxygen
machine to Janet's bedside and held the mask to
her face, assuring Morna and her mother that all
would be well. When Janet's breathing seemed
easier, they gently carried her to the ambulance,
and off they sped to the hospital.

They were critical minutes, and frightening
ones. For until the ambulance men arrived so
swiftly, Morna and her mother thought they had
lost Janet. How proud I am to raise my hat to the
two men, and the unsung heroes like them, who,
somewhere in the night, are helping save the life of
someone like Janet.

WEDNESDAY—APRIL 9.

*IT'S only those who weep sometimes
    Who find that life is sweet;
It's only tired folk whose rest
    Is dreamless and complete.
And only those who give and give
Can claim they know how best to live.*

THE FRIENDSHIP BOOK

LOOKING through some yellowed cuttings I came upon an item which intrigued me.

It was about a book written during the last war by Hans Olav and Tor Myklebost, and it was intended to cheer everybody and help them to endure bravely.

Four words in the book struck me. They are a sermon and a challenge—and if you are finding the going hard just now, and are tempted to give in, perhaps they will help you to keep on.

The four words are—*He who laughs . . . lasts.*

JENNIE THRELFALL'S parents died while she was still a little girl. She found a home with an uncle and aunt—then they, too, died.

But their married daughter came to Jennie's rescue, and she went to London to live with her and her husband. There she met with an accident that turned her into a helpless invalid.

It would have been so easy for Jennie to look around bitterly at the happiness of others and compare their blessings with her misfortunes. But she accepted her lot without complaint, and she was beloved by all who knew her. It was with her the children shared their secrets; it was she who listened to their problems.

And, though they may not know it, children still remember Jennie every Easter, for it was this crippled orphan girl who wrote—

Hosanna, loud hosanna, the little children sang;

Nothing, I'm sure, would have made Jennie happier than to think children's voices would still be singing her hymn 100 years after she had gone.

SATURDAY—APRIL 12.

JIMMY'S mother wore a worried look one after-noon as she said to her son, aged seven—" The cat hasn't come in for his dinner yet, and it's nearly four o'clock. I hope nothing's happened to him."

Trying to comfort his mother, Jimmy said cheer-fully, " Oh, he'll be all right, Mum. He didn't come in yesterday till this morning, so he may not come back today till tomorrow."

SUNDAY—APRIL 13.

GOD is not a man, that He should lie.

MONDAY—APRIL 14.

A HYMN which has long been a favourite of mine is, " Thou Hidden Love of God, Whose Height . . ." When I hear it my mind goes back over the centuries to a little shop in a German town. Behind the counter worked a lad of 16 called Gerhard Tersteegen—and, young as he was, he was haunted by the poverty around him.

So one day he gave up his job, found a tumble-down cottage on the outskirts of the town, and set up an old loom to weave silk ribbons. He ate only one meal a day and all the money he saved from the sale of his ribbons he gave to the poor.

As his fame spread, Gerhard's simple home became known as the " Pilgrim's Cottage," for troubled folk flocked to it from far and near.

But he never left his cottage, and when he died there at 72 he was still a poor man. Yet who can deny that he left behind him, in this one great hymn, a splendid legacy to us all—

Then shall my heart from earth be free,
When it has found repose in Thee . . .

TUESDAY—APRIL 15.

ONE Sunday afternoon, 43 silent men stepped through the doors of St Machar's Cathedral, Aberdeen. They were Russian seamen from a ship that had called at the harbour, and now they were being shown the sights of the city.

As they moved through the kirk, the beadle came forward to meet them. He told them a christening service was about to take place and, though it had been planned as a simple family ceremony, they were invited to join in.

The men were intrigued, for they were Communists and had never witnessed a christening. So Albert led them to the front of the kirk and showed them into the pews beside the family of the baby.

Most of the Russians couldn't understand a word that was said, but all realised the significance of what was taking place. They watched spellbound as the minister took the child in his arms and sprinkled its head with water.

Though the Russians had probably never prayed in their lives before, every man among them bowed his head as the minister asked for God's blessing on the child.

Oh, these Russian sailors saw many grand sights in Aberdeen that day—but I'm sure the memory that will stay with them longest will be of the little service they shared in St Machar's.

WEDNESDAY—APRIL 16.

THE stars like jewels shine at night,
The Alps are crowned with snow;
How wonderful a springtime wood,
A field where daisies grow.
But to the housewife what's so fine
As her washing drying on the line?

THURSDAY—APRIL 17.

FAITH, as seen through the eyes of others.

You can do very little with it, but you can do nothing without it.—Samuel Butler.

It is the heart which experiences God, and not the reason. This, then, is faith: God felt by the heart, not by the reason.—Pascal.

Faith is the soul riding at anchor.—Josh Billings.

Faith means not wanting to know what is true. —Friedrich Nietzsche.

Faith in our associates is part of our faith in God.—Charles Horton Cooley.

FRIDAY—APRIL 18.

TWO men set out from the village of Muirkirk to make a pilgrimage over the Ayrshire hills.

They were Mr Wm. Stirling and Mr Walter Storrar. They were searching for the lonely grave of a Covenanter named William Adam who was killed in 1685.

For, though both are getting on in years, they have vowed to do all they can to search out the memorials of the Covenanters, and clean and repair them.

Some of the graves are in the kirkyards. Others are in hidden places among the hills, where faithful souls had gathered and where they were shot down as they worshipped. Indeed, William and Walter had almost lost hope of discovering the grave they were looking for when suddenly they saw it on the edge of a wood on the far side of the river. Undaunted, they rolled up their trouser legs, and waded across to the other bank. There, reverently, they cleaned the stone and repaired the lettering.

Are they living in the past? I don't think so. I salute the pilgrims—for, in a way, they are trying to repay a debt that is nearly 300 years old.

THE FRIENDSHIP BOOK

SATURDAY—APRIL 19.

HOW curious it is that so few of us do as we say or follow the advice we give. We expect others to be honest, but are apt to find an excuse for being just a little less than honest ourselves—some extenuating circumstances excuse us.

Most of us find it easier to quote a precept than to set a good example; and all of us know that Shakespeare himself declared—*If to do were as easy as to know what were good to do, chapels had been churches and poor men's cottages princes' palaces. It is a good divine that follows his own instructions. I can easier teach twenty what were good to be done than be one of the twenty to follow mine own teaching.*

All of which should help to make us a little more sympathetic and a little less critical when some one we know makes a mistake or falls from grace.

SUNDAY—APRIL 20.

MAN doth not live by bread only, but by every word that proceedeth out of the mouth of the Lord doth man live.

MONDAY—APRIL 21.

RECENTLY Steve Sloan, football quarter-back of Alabama University in U.S.A., said something really important.

It had nothing to do with football.

I mention it because it is a tremendous challenge to you and me, and because, if we kept his few words in mind, our lives might be finer than they are.

This is what Steve said—*You should be able to recognise a Christian merely by looking at him.*

Worth thinking about, isn't it?

TUESDAY—APRIL 22.

HE was one of the thousands of folk from all over the country who packed the arena at Earls Court, London, to listen to Dr Billy Graham. What he heard stirred him deeply.

So much so that, after the meeting, he found his way to the back of the arena and asked if he could see Billy Graham. When he was invited in, he explained he was a prisoner on parole from Manchester Jail, and that what he heard that night had made him resolve to live a better life.

But, he went on, if Dr Graham's message could do that for him, could it not also help the men who were still in prison? That is why he had summoned up his courage to see Billy Graham—for he wanted his help in arranging with the Governor to bring a whole busload of prisoners to one of his meetings.

Well, heads were put together, phone calls were made, permission was sought and granted. A few days later a bus left Manchester filled with prisoners and their warders, all in plain clothes, bound for London. When they arrived they filed quietly into the seats at Earls Court that had been reserved for them, and heard the thrilling message that has changed the lives of so many.

No one, of course, can say what the outcome of all this will be, but it is worth remembering that no harvest was ever reaped without sowing seed . . .

WEDNESDAY—APRIL 23.

THE world is big and I am small—
Just simply nobody at all.
MY world is small, but if I try
I CAN do something by and by
To share a burden, bring a smile,
Or help someone to climb a stile.

OUT OF THE SHADOWS

Keep head and heart uplifted,
Though all is grey below;
For, high upon the hilltops,
The morning sun's aglow.

DAVID HOPE

WORKING TOGETHER

We're working hard, me and my mum,
Helped a bit by little brother,
Stacking peats and having fun
And glad to be with one another.

DAVID HOPE

THURSDAY—APRIL 24.

THOUGH these words are simple, they are also telling, and I pass them on to all who believe that a mother's good example is a child's finest gift:—

A careful mother I must be
To the little one who follows me.
I dare not ever go astray
For fear she'll go the self-same way.
Remember—what she sees me do,
She might, herself, try one day, too.
She must believe I'm good and fine,
For she'll accept each word of mine.
A fault in me she must not see—
For I build for the years to be

FRIDAY—APRIL 25.

THE old cleaner took me round the church, showing me the silken pulpit frontal, the fitted carpets, the fresh hangings round the chancel, and where the " beautiful stained glass " window had been removed, which darkened the building rather than letting in God's good daylight. " We did it all ourselves," she said, " and we've cleared off every penny of the cost."

Over in the manse the minister told me a different story; how the alterations had been carried out on the advice of the best architects and designers, but in the teeth of local opposition. Now they are so proud of the improvements—as at last they see them to be—that they not only tell their friends, but take the credit, too.

Things with which we have grown too familiar can be dusty, or moth-eaten and faded. We should therefore always be prepared to keep our minds open to fresh ideas.

SATURDAY—APRIL 26.

IT was late at night when we came upon the road accident, and although neither was killed, two men were injured. How it came about I'm not too sure, but presently I found myself at the hospital carrying a specimen of blood across to the laboratory for " cross grouping and matching," while one of those hurt was being prepared for the theatre.

The sleepy technician in the laboratory looked at the blood specimen, saying—" It's this fairly uncommon type, I guess, and I have only this one pint in the frig. But I must be sure." It was more than an hour before all his checks were completed.

A strange place, indeed, to find myself in the middle of the night! During all that time I was thinking of the thousands of men and women who freely give their blood, so that those injured in accidents or those undergoing surgery for any other reason may live.

SUNDAY—APRIL 27.

SPEAK, Lord; for Thy servant heareth.

MONDAY—APRIL 28.

THE late Dr James Black, a former minister of St George's West Church in Edinburgh, wrote:—" There are no inferior people to whom we can graciously unbend or condescend. There are, of course, vulgar and common people everywhere in every so-called grade of society, but the worst vulgarity of all is the vulgarity of conceit, pride, affectation, vanity, the arrogance of riches and the insolence of intellect. I praise God that Jesus gave His finest blessing to the ' meek and lowly,' those who are essentially humble of heart."

TUESDAY—APRIL 29.

NEARLY 100 years ago, a young American singer and composer sat in his room, idly looking over some verses that had been sent to him.

His name was Hart Danks—and, as he scanned the verses, he felt his heart quicken. For they spoke to him of all he felt for his own wife, of the comfort they would be to each other when they grew old.

There and then he took up his pen and began to write the tune he already heard in his mind—and when he had finished, the words and music of a famous song were lying on his desk.

> Darling, I am growing old.
> Silver threads among the gold,
> Shine upon my brow today,
> Life is fading fast away . . .

A lovely song, and I would like to tell you that, for Danks and his wife in their old age, all that it promised came true. Alas, it was not to be. They parted, and for the last 30 years of his life he was a lonely, broken man.

His life ended in a Philadelphia boarding-house in 1903, and when he was found by his landlady, a copy of his song was beside him. On it he had written, " It is hard to die alone . . ."

Perhaps, in a way, his own tragic story helps us to see the truth in his song's great message—where there is love, the flowers can never fade.

WEDNESDAY—APRIL 30.

> MAYBE, when young, you just can't give
>   Big sums to some good cause;
> But can you not afford, at times,
>   In busy days to pause
> To share with someone, old and grey,
> The sunshine of your happy day?

MAY

SOMEHOW I had always imagined the writer of the hymn "Who Is On The Lord's Side?" to be a man of action—one who had gone forward with the sword of faith to win battles for his Maker. Yet it was written by a frail girl called Frances Havergal.

All her life she suffered from poor health. Even as a little girl she was delicate, and she found consolation in writing lines of poetry. In a way it was a blessing that it was so, for before she died at only 43 she had given us hymns like " Golden Harps Are Sounding," " Like A River Glorious," and " Take My Life And Let It Be."

But, to me, the finest of them all is the hymn I shall never sing without saluting her memory—

Fierce may be the conflict,
Strong may be the foe . . .

THESE lines, which I heard the other day, may be of comfort in time of sorrow:—

He giveth more grace as our burdens grow greater, He sendeth more strength as our labours increase; to added afflictions He addeth His mercy, to multiplied trials He multiplies peace.

When we have exhausted our store of endurance, when our strength has failed ere the day is half done; when we reach the end of our humble resources, His bountiful giving is only begun.

His love has no limits, His grace has no measure, His power no boundary known unto men; from out of His infinite mercy and riches, He giveth, and giveth, and giveth again.

SATURDAY—MAY 3.

MARY HEWITT'S a pensioner, always on the look-out for someone she can help. One Friday night she was busy going round with a tin, collecting on behalf of the Guide Dogs for the Blind. She was getting on fine, too, when she came to the door of the Cockatoo Bar.

Now Mary, bless her, had never been in a pub in her life—but why not? she asked herself. So she pushed open the door and in she went. The men were surprised to see her, and Mary wondered if she'd done the right thing. Then a voice called out, " Why don't you give us a song, love?"

Undaunted, Mary drew a deep breath and launched into a hymn. You could have heard a pin drop. When it ended, the applause was deafening—indeed, they wouldn't let Mary go until she'd sung an encore, " I'll Walk Beside You."

The upshot was that Mary's tin was filled to overflowing. I'm sure if there were more folk like Mary, ready to venture into the unknown and prepared to do anything for a good cause, there'd be a lot less want and sorrow in this old world.

SUNDAY—MAY 4.

GOD said, Let there be light : and there was light.

MONDAY—MAY 5.

I HEAR that Jane, aged six, is finding school irksome these days, and I can sympathise with her if there is just a hint of envy in a remark she made recently to her grandparents. After meditating at the tea table, she sighed deeply and remarked with feeling—" Why can't I just stay at home every day and get a pension as you do?"

TUESDAY—MAY 6.

PERHAPS from time to time we all need to be reminded of these things—

Don't tell a little fib—it leads to telling lies.

Don't envy others—you'll soon grow bitter and discontented.

Don't forgive yourself too easily—you'll become too critical of others and be without friends.

Don't do small, mean things—you'll be shunned.

Do remember that many years ago a wise man wrote:—*No one ever reaches the depths of wickedness all at once.*

WEDNESDAY—MAY 7.

NOW, the way to be happy is this:—
Get on with the job you must do.
Better be red with exertion and toil
Than moaning because you feel blue !

THURSDAY—MAY 8.

THESE words are being scribbled at a greater height than Francis Gay ever wrote for you before—on board one of the latest jet airliners at a height of nearly thirty thousand feet and flying at well over five hundred miles per hour. Coming on board, the first thing that one notices is the welcome extended to all passengers, not only by the pretty air hostess, but by the captain himself, speaking over the loudspeaker. Special care is taken with children and old people.

Here we sit, the Lady of the House and myself, having a meal, and asking one another if this new form of transport has not recaptured a form of courtesy that some older ways of transport may have lost.

FRIDAY—MAY 9.

I VISITED a nursery garden the other day and found myself thinking what a wonderful way it was to have one's name remembered as the name for a special rose: as Ena Harkness or General McArthur (crimson), Mrs Sam McGredy (orange), or Violet Carson (salmon).

Surely there is no other gift costing only a few shillings which gives such pleasure as a present of a rose bush! A shrub rose, with good fortune, may live and grow larger and more lovely every year for a century. Quite enormous bushes they can be, too, in the gardens of some of the great estates which are now so often open to the public.

The gardener who planted these may be long gone, but it is perfectly possible that in some far-off sphere he may know that his planting and his care still bring joy to many.

SATURDAY—MAY 10.

JUST as some small boys will " collect " railway engines or car numbers, so a certain bishop collects the more unusual names of public-houses. I am sure that the bishop would prefer me not to give his name.

He had forgotten his hobby when he arrived in some haste at an important garden fete in his diocese, just in time to play his part at the official opening. But his daughter, Janice (11), was well prepared to keep her distinguished father up to scratch. All the local celebrities were present in the tea tent when there came one of those pauses and hubbub of conversation suddenly died away. It was this moment Janice chose to expostulate—"Daddy, we came here far too fast. We missed five good pubs in that last place!"

SUNDAY—MAY 11.

TO every thing there is a season, and a time to every purpose under the heaven.

MONDAY—MAY 12.

A FRIEND, just home from the U.S.A., tells me of one of the highlights of his business trip to New York.

It was a visit to a large office where hundreds of employees seemed to be working for dear life.

" One of our biggest difficulties with staff," the manager explained to my friend, " is promotion. We've just got to keep on promoting because girls will marry or men will die and leave a vacancy to fill or, in fact, by promoting Bill we have to promote Jack to take his place. And the trouble with newly-promoted people is that often they feel more important than they are."

" So what ?" my friend asked.

The American manager grinned pleasantly. " We give every promotee a little present—a book on business methods. And on the fly-leaf we write the warning — *The bigger your head becomes, the easier it is for us to fill your shoes.*

The manager added—" It nearly always works."

TUESDAY—MAY 13.

I FEEL there is a good deal to challenge us in these four simple lines —
To each is given a bag of tools,
An hour glass and a book of rules;
And each must build, ere his time be flown,
A stumbling block or a stepping stone.
The question is — which will you and I leave behind us ?

THE HEART OF THINGS

Find the centre of this, the centre of that,
Ask me such questions — I simply fall flat!
But one thing is easy, the answer is clear:
The centre of life is the folks we hold dear.

DAVID HOPE

ALL AS ONE

Take the strain and h-h-heave
Till your muscles crack!
Now altogether lads,
Back, and back and back.

When life's strain is on
And we're short of hope,
May we always have
Friends upon the rope!

DAVID HOPE

POOR MOTHER

I've brought them this, I've brought them that,
*   They've surely had their fill;*
But now I'm back again and look!
*   They're just as hungry still.*

DAVID HOPE

THE FRIENDSHIP BOOK

WEDNESDAY—MAY 14.

B LESSED be the friend who calls one day,
  And helps wash up and clear away;
Who needs no formal invitation,
Polite small talk or conversation.
She is an angel in disguise
With love and laughter in her eyes!

THURSDAY—MAY 15.

YEARS ago a young Scotsman left his native Edinburgh to seek his fortune on the other side of the Atlantic.

His father had devoted his life to helping deaf and dumb children, and now he, too, had dedicated himself to the same work, for he had seen so often what a terrible handicap deafness could be. When he reached Boston, the town that was to become his home, he threw himself into his work.

Perhaps he was spurred on by his love for one of his pupils, a beautiful, deaf girl called Mabel Hubbard. If he could help her to hear again, it would be the greatest gift he could give her.

Be that as it may, his early experiments with the hearing aids helped the young Scot to stumble on something that literally changed the world. For his name was Alexander Graham Bell, and it was at his work bench that he realised he could not only help the deaf to hear, but give men the power to speak to one another even though they were thousands of miles apart. Yes, he had found the secret of the telephone.

Well, a few years later, Alexander Graham Bell married Mabel, and as soon as he saw his telephone launched on the road to success, he left it to others and went back to the work that was closest to his heart — helping deaf folk.

THE FRIENDSHIP BOOK

FRIDAY—MAY 16.

MEETING a friend, I heard about his visit to a large business concern, where he had met and lunched with the managing director. " And what kind of a man is he ?" I inquired.

" Well," was the reply, " I can speak of him only as I found him, and I was in his company less than two hours. But he was friendly, easy to get on with, and apparently straight as they make them." My acquaintance hesitated. " Difficult to say more," he mused aloud. " I'd say he is the kind of man who always walks on the sunny side of the street."

That, I felt, was enough. I think I should like to know a man like that.

SATURDAY—MAY 17.

THE Glasgow Police Pipe Band went to Salerno, in Italy, to attend a musical festival there.

One afternoon, as the bobbies were sitting in a cafe at the roadside, one of them remembered there was a war cemetery near Salerno. Wouldn't it be a fine thing, he suggested, if they were to visit it and pay tribute to the lads who lie there ?

So they went back to their hotel and changed into full regalia. Then they marched to the cemetery where 2000 men of the Black Watch, Seaforths, Scots Guards, Fleet Air Arm, and R.N.V.R. are buried.

They halted in a clearing in the middle of the cemetery and there, while the rest of the band stood to attention, Pipe-Major Ronald Lawrie stepped forward and began to play " The Flowers o' The Forest." As the haunting notes skirled away over the countryside, it seemed even the very birds had paused in their song, so deep was the stillness.

Yes, a proud and splendid salute.

THE FRIENDSHIP BOOK

THE path of the just is as the shining light, that shineth more and more unto the perfect day.

MONDAY—MAY 19.

VERY often the less important a person is, the bigger the notions he has of himself.

The story is going the rounds of an Edinburgh solicitor who got chatting with a message boy. " And what's your name ?" he asked.

" Robert Bruce," was the reply—chin up as it was said.

The solicitor, with a twinkle in his eye, murmured, " Well now, is that so ? That's a pretty famous name."

The message boy was evidently pleased. " Sure," he purred, all smiles. " It ought to be ! I've been delivering groceries around this district for two years now."

TUESDAY—MAY 20.

DID you hear about wee Susan who asked her father—" What does L on a car mean ?"

Her father explained that it told people the driver was a learner.

A day or two later Susan spotted a car with GB in large letters. " Oh," she exclaimed, " that car has a learner who is Getting Better !"

The thought occurred to me that while learning to drive is a tricky business, learning to live successfully is even more difficult. It's a long process, too. It's fine to change a Learner for a Getting Better (as Susan thought), but in life, however young or old we are, it's our job to ensure that our good is better and our better best !

THE FRIENDSHIP BOOK

WEDNESDAY—MAY 21.

*FORGIVE my boast, but I must say
        I walked a mile this sunny day;
A mile! A mile! Just think of it—
A mile I walked without one sit!
I'm well and strong, but some I know
Not even HALF a mile can go;
Nor see the fields and woods so gay
Which I looked on this sunny day!*

THURSDAY—MAY 22.

I THINK there's a lot we can learn from this little story.

Mrs Gordon leads a busy life as a lady of the manse, yet she still makes time to wheel a trolley of library books round wards in the local infirmary on Tuesday afternoons.

Recently one old lady stumped her. Mrs Gordon suggested she might enjoy a light novel—a romance, perhaps, or a mystery story. " No, thank you," the old lady replied, " I want a book about the Incas of Peru!"

She went on to explain she read nothing else but books on travel and exploration. She'd never been far beyond her native town, but through the books she read she had journeyed to the depths of the African jungle, trekked through India and Burma, sailed up the Nile and crossed the Sahara Desert, penetrated China, visited the South Sea Islands, and struggled through blizzards to the North and South Poles. " Yes," she smiled, " I've travelled the world from my bed."

I can't help feeling that if at times your life seems dull and grey, the example of this old lady may help you to realise there are countless doors through which you may venture to new worlds.

<u>FRIDAY—MAY 23.</u>

ADVERTISED in the paper as a holiday house to be let by the month, it seemed to be particularly attractive. So Murdo, who has a large family, rang up the advertiser. " You will have to go at the end of the queue," said the distant voice. " I'm afraid I've had dozens of inquiries."

Murdo was telling me about it later. " I thought I noticed a strong Highland accent," he told me, " so I gave him a word or two in the Gaelic."

" Well, now, that's different," said the advertiser. " We'll put you down for the month of August, seeing you have the Gaelic !"

They do say, and it's true, I think, that all Highlanders are clannish. But " clan " is a Gaelic word meaning simply " family," so what started off as a business transaction became just a family arrangement !

<u>SATURDAY—MAY 24.</u>

WHEN you are getting on in years it's pleasant recalling happy days long gone by.

Delightful now and then to search the memory and recall some lively adventure, some party, some chance meeting, some hilarious moment that seems to live for ever. Delightful, also, to remember some of the hardships we endured and the triumphs over trouble which were ours.

And whatever is wrong now, how good to live again a day when everything was right !

This thought, I feel sure, was in Leigh Hunt's mind when, over a century ago, he wrote:—

Say I'm weary, say I'm sad;
    Say that health and wealth have missed me;
Say I'm growing old, but add—
    Jenny kissed me !

SUNDAY—MAY 25.

WISDOM is the principal thing; therefore get wisdom : and with all thy getting get understanding.

MONDAY—MAY 26.

MANY of us are greatly concerned about the times in which we live, and it is highly desirable that we should be so—there are enough dangers and undesirable tendencies to disturb us.

Even so, I could not help smiling, if perhaps a trifle sadly, at the words of a much-too-cheery optimist who declared only the other day:—*This is a wonderful generation to belong to. Everything wrong is the fault of the stupid people who came before us, and it will have to be put right by the generation which comes after us.*

Happily, quite a lot of folk don't look at life that way.

TUESDAY—MAY 27.

I SAT down to write half an hour ago. Rain was falling from a grey sky. The room was cheerless. I did not look out of the window very often but concentrated on my job.

All at once I became aware of change. I glanced from my writing, realising that the rain was over and gone, that the sky had patches of blue and that the sun was pouring in at the window, filling the room with light and warmth, and making even my untidy table top bright.

However dull life may be for you . . . keep going, do what has to be done, try not to be too discouraged or disconsolate—the sun will shine again for you !

THE FRIENDSHIP BOOK

IMAGINE life's a dull affair
And all folk are unkind,
A poor world this will be for you—
The trouble's in your mind.
Believe this world has goodness in it—
Then you'll find sunshine in each minute.

THURSDAY—MAY 29.

IT is many years since Jimmy Simpson was born in Bathgate. He was the son of the village baker, the youngest of seven boys. When he was four, he went to the local school and it wasn't long before the dominie knew that young Jimmy was the brightest pupil he would ever have.

In those days, of course, there were no college grants or scholarships. If a boy wanted to go to university, his family had to find every penny by themselves. But, without hesitation, Jimmy's father and his six brothers decided that no matter how hard a struggle it would be, they would help the boy to go to university in Edinburgh.

How richly they were rewarded. In 1832, at 21, Jimmy became a fully qualified doctor. At only 24, he was elected president of the Royal Medical Society of Edinburgh. At 28, he became a professor.

But his greatest achievement and one for which he is still remembered, was that he discovered how to use chloroform as an anæsthetic—for Jimmy Simpson, the baker's boy, became none other than Sir James Young Simpson, one of the greatest doctors of all time.

Today, the names of his six selfless brothers are forgotten—but who can doubt that their part in giving the blessing of chloroform to the world was, in its own way, just as important as Jimmy's?

FRIDAY—MAY 30.

MOTHER CARTY, who lives in California and is well turned 90, has a sweet disposition and a serenity born of a deep faith.

Some of us, troubled by the insecurity of the world today may wish we could say, as she says, towards the close of a long life —

> At cool of day with God I walk
> My garden's grateful shade.
> I hear his voice among the trees,
> And I am not afraid.

SATURDAY—MAY 31.

A FARMER recently told me of a weird experience of his boyhood.

One Sunday, in winter, he had been at his aunt's house three miles from the farm where he lived. It was a windy night as he marched cheerily homeward in the darkness, his lamp swinging in his hand. Then he slipped and his lamp went out.

Born and bred in the country, the boy was no coward. But after picking himself up and walking warily he heard sounds he could not account for— like distant voices on the rising wind, ghostly calls from nowhere. He paused, transfixed, listening intently, wondering whether what he heard was nothing but imagination or the voice of foe or friend.

Suddenly he saw a light moving. For a moment he was terrified. Then he heard his father's voice saying: " Your mother thought I'd better come along to meet you, lad."

All was well.

I rather think you and I sometimes feel a bit like that scared boy, for we seem lost in the darkness ... but if we hear a voice or see a light, we know this is God's world, and all's well.

GUESSING

I've never been to Coleman's Hatch,
Nor yet to Forest Row.
They make me think of country ways
And hay that's ripe to mow.
Are they all the names suggest?
Perhaps one day I'll know.
I'll say hullo to Coleman's Hatch
And look up Forest Row.

DAVID HOPE

LEARNING

Holiday time — they'll run and climb,
  Dip in a lonely pool,
In nature's class learn lessons
  They'd never learn at school.

DAVID HOPE

JUNE

THEN shall the lame man leap as an hart, and the tongue of the dumb sing; for in the wilderness shall waters break out, and streams in the desert.

MONDAY—JUNE 2.

WULLIE McVEY has been a miner since he started work over fifty years ago.

Indeed, it's the family tradition, for his seven brothers were miners, and so are his two sons.

Every day Wullie cycled six miles to the colliery and at the end of his shift he cycled the six miles back home again. It was a hard and often dangerous life, but Wullie wouldn't have changed it for the world.

Then, one Friday, he cycled to the pit for the last time, for he was retiring at the end of his shift. When the day's work was over, he took a last look at the place where he'd worked for so long, then turned to his old bike for his final journey home.

To his surprise, he found his way barred by a band of his miner friends. " No bike for you today, Wullie," they smiled. " You're going home in style !" And there, waiting specially for him, was a big, shiny Rolls-Royce, complete with a uniformed chauffeur.

So, to a cheer from his mates and a bow from the chauffeur, Wullie stepped into the Rolls, and made his journey home in state.

You know, I can't think of anyone who more deserves to be treated like a king than Wullie, who for fifty years and more has helped to keep the home fires burning !

THE FRIENDSHIP BOOK

<u>TUESDAY—JUNE 3.</u>

SOME years ago a little girl lay gravely ill. The doctor had done all he could, but now he told her mother that only a miracle could save her.

He was overheard by the girl's brother, a wee boy of five. Straight away he went to his piggy-bank and emptied out its contents—six pennies, a silver threepenny, and a foreign coin. Then he slipped out of the house, and along the road to the chemist's shop. There he asked the chemist for a ninepenny miracle, please.

The chemist, a good man, was puzzled. " Why do you want it, son ?" he asked. The little boy repeated what the doctor had said, and the chemist understood. " I'm sorry," he said kindly. " We don't have that kind of miracle here."

But a stranger in the shop overheard the boy's story. He asked him where he lived, then they set off together down the street and into the house where the girl lay. The man told the weeping mother that he was a surgeon, and asked to see the little girl. A few moments later, he looked up and said, " Madam, I believe I can save her." So he wrapped her in a blanket, called his car, and took her to hospital. It was touch and go—but he saved her life.

That is the story of the ninepenny miracle—and somewhere in it there is a message that can speak to the heart of every one of us.

<u>WEDNESDAY—JUNE 4.</u>

A THOUSAND days has June for me,
*   A thousand days, and more;*
June's song and sun, June's scents and fun,
*   It's loveliness galore . . .*
All these, like every bee that hums,
I store for days when winter comes !

THURSDAY—JUNE 5.

LEAVING the Army with the rank of sergeant-major, the only suitable job that Peter Borthwick could find was that of a security guard. It meant long hours, working almost every night, guarding banks or industrial premises. The pay was smaller than his Army pay. But Peter Borthwick put his heart into the job. His wife grumbled, and, any other woman would say, not without cause!

Just the other morning she came almost running in the door. "Mrs Gay," she called, "he's been promoted! A car of his own, shorter hours, higher pay." All this within the space of a year. If you do a humble job well, the reward may come sooner and more suddenly than you expect.

FRIDAY—JUNE 6.

WHEN Nurse Brown unexpectedly came into a bit of money, she decided to leave the hospital.

Friends said she was crazy when she bought a house in a village miles from anywhere. They declared she would be lonely and unable to fill her days, especially after such a busy life.

But Nurse Brown knew what she was doing. Before she had got her bits of furniture to rights, word went round the village she was a trained nurse. First the doctor, then the minister called to see her; and when a farmer, a mile or two off, had a thrombosis, Nurse Brown was asked to help.

Within two months she was part and parcel of the village—known to every mother and child, helping here and there . . . Why, she was as busy in retirement as she had ever been when a sister in the wards.

Which suited her fine . . . and reminds me that where you are counts for little. It's what you are.

SATURDAY—JUNE 7.

THE first rose of summer always reminds me of something said once by a wise old gardener—

" A lot of folk grumble because God put thorns on roses, but I think it's better to thank Him for putting roses on thorns."

That, to me, seems to sum up an attitude to life that can make many a dull day brighter.

SUNDAY—JUNE 8.

O THOU of little faith, wherefore didst thou doubt?

MONDAY—JUNE 9.

" WHILE women weep, as they do now, I'll fight.

" While little children go hungry, as they do now, I'll fight.

" While men go to prison, in and out, in and out, I'll fight.

" While there is a drunkard left, while there is a poor, lost girl on the streets, while there remains one dark soul without the light of God, I'll fight—I'll fight to the very end !"

Surely, you say, this can only be the declaration of a young man on the threshold of life, dedicating himself to the work that is waiting to be done.

But it is no such thing. It is the testimony of a frail, old man of 83, almost blind and in failing health, spoken a few weeks before he died in 1912.

He was William Booth, founder of the Salvation Army—and who can doubt that, down through the years, those words have echoed like a trumpet-call in the hearts of the men and women who have carried on his glorious battle ?

TUESDAY—JUNE 10.

MORE than 100 years ago a young American minister lay dying.

He had been a stirring preacher, speaking out fearlessly against slavery and, because many members of his congregation owned slaves, he was forced to resign from his church. But he went on preaching until, soon after, he was badly injured in an accident.

Now he was dying, and beside him sat another minister, Rev. George Duffield, who had stood by him through thick and thin. Just before the end the dying man looked up at his friend and whispered, " Tell them to stand up for Jesus !"

They were the last words he ever spoke and they haunted the man to whom they were spoken. That night, again and again, he found himself repeating them—and, at length, he took up a pen and paper and began to write the lines that sprang almost unbidden to his lips.

When he had finished, he decided to read them at his friend's funeral service, and it was in this way that the world heard for the first time a hymn that, ever since, has thrilled the hearts of all who sing it:—

> Stand up, stand up for Jesus,
> Ye soldiers of the Cross;
> Lift high His royal banner,
> It must not suffer loss . . .

WEDNESDAY—JUNE 11.

> *SO many things can break your heart,*
> *So cruel life can be;*
> *You lose all hope, all joy is gone,*
> *The way you cannot see.*
> *But if you grope through tragic night,*
> *There breaks, at last, the morning light !*

THURSDAY—JUNE 12.

IN London's Hyde Park there is a memorial to him—a bird sanctuary, and although his name is fading (he died in 1922) and his books are less read than formerly, he remains a striking and challenging and elusive personality.

He was William Henry Hudson, born in Argentina, and remembered as one of the greatest of all naturalists, an amateur with an amazing knowledge of wild life, of birds and animals—and, indeed, of men and women.

On his grave are the famous words:—He loved birds and green places and the wind upon the heath, and saw the brightness of the skirts of God.

I feel that at this season of the year when fields and woods and lanes and gardens are at their best, you and I ought not to let their glory pass without somehow making time to be alone in green places.

FRIDAY—JUNE 13.

GRANDPA PARKSON takes it all as his due. Jennifer, his married daughter, helps him in every way that she can. She also has the worries of her own daughter Mary, married eighteen months ago and now complete with her first baby. Mr Parkson is therefore made into a great-grand-father.

It is easy to lay demands on those of middle years, and whether as sons or fathers, whether as daughters or mothers, they will do as much as they can and maybe more. A great deal is said about the needs of the elderly, and almost as much about the care of the young. Perhaps all the other age-groups might sometimes take a thought for the middle-aged who, however willing, are no longer as fit as they were.

THE FRIENDSHIP BOOK

SATURDAY—JUNE 14.

THESE lines were written about a very new wife, but I think some " old hands " at the baking game will agree that things can go wrong even in the best-regulated homes.

She measured out the butter with a very solemn air, the milk and sugar also, and she took the greatest care to count the eggs correctly and to add that little bit of baking powder which, you know, beginners oft omit. Then she mixed them all together, and she baked it for an hour—but she never quite forgave herself for leaving out the flour.

SUNDAY—JUNE 15.

WHEN thou doest alms, let not thy left hand know what thy right hand doeth.

MONDAY—JUNE 16.

I AM all for work—hard work, and plenty of it. Hard work never killed anybody.

And yet, having said all this, I believe that Chinese philosopher, Lin You Tang, has the truth of the matter in him when he says:—When you have spent a perfectly useless afternoon in a perfectly useless way, you have learnt how to live.

He is right. Work is excellent. But there is something more in life. Now and again it is good for the spirit to do nothing, attempt nothing, relax, look, listen, dream—opening a window of the soul, as it were, to the timeless things that make for our enrichment and give us poise as we go about whatever tasks the day may bring.

Work and work hard. Be busy.

But do nothing sometimes.

TUESDAY—JUNE 17.

A FEW years ago Rev. Alex. McIlvean was a busy minister. Then his sight began to fail, and he was warned he must prepare for the day when he would be all but blind, for it seemed an operation would not have helped him then.

It was a bitter blow, but the minister accepted it bravely and carried on with his work. After 18 months he could no longer see to read or write. Sadly he decided to seek a smaller parish, where he could serve his flock fully, despite his handicap.

He found it on the island of Coll, where his new congregation numbered only 25. He was almost blind, but the islanders did all they could to help him, and, in return, he brought them blessing. Indeed, as they watched him week by week and listened to him declare his faith, they could not but be strengthened by his message.

Then, recently, Mr McIlvean underwent the operation he had waited for so patiently. When the bandages were removed from his eyes, he found he could see again dimly. Now the sight in his right eye is almost perfect.

That is why he has now bid farewell to his beloved congregation in Coll. For he believes God restored his sight because there was a bigger task waiting for him.

May he have every happiness and success.

WEDNESDAY—JUNE 18.

*Y*OU'RE *kind, you say? I'm glad of that—*
    It warms my heart no end;
I'm SURE you have a ready smile,
    A willing hand to lend.
You'll carry on? I KNOW you will . . .
    And be a little kinder still!

THE FRIENDSHIP BOOK

WHEN we arrived home recently after seeing a young friend of ours married, the Lady of the House said to me, " Francis, why does a bride cut her wedding cake at the reception ?"

Frankly, I had no idea. Later, however, a minister friend gave us the answer. It's simply that cutting the cake is the first thing a bride ever does for her husband after they are married !

Oh, I know the modern fashion is for the 'groom to help his bride to cut the cake. But, in the old days, the bride used to bake the wedding cake herself—and when she cut it, she handed the first piece to her husband. It was almost as if, in doing so, she promised that from then on he would always come first in her life.

Rather a fine old tradition, wasn't it ?

FROM one of the biggest cities in Russia comes the story of how, last century, a main thoroughfare was to be extended, and the contractors were at their wits end to know how to remove an immense mass of rock which blocked the way. Using dynamite was too risky. At that time pneumatic drills were unknown, and though the rock could have been broken up, the cost would have been enormous.

Eventually a farmer came along, and offered to remove the rock. He was as good as his word. He engaged workmen who dug a hole and carried off the soil. At last, when all was ready, a small charge of dynamite was enough to topple the rock into the hole. And there it lies to this day.

How very true it is that sometimes we rack our brains to find a difficult solution to our problem while all the time there is a simple way out.

SATURDAY—JUNE 21.

LONG years ago a young lad used to help in a blacksmith's shop. It was hard, for in those days a smiddy was a busy place. One of the boy's jobs was to shape the blades of the ploughs—and you can imagine the massive blows needed for that.

But the blacksmith allowed the boy to strike only a few of these mighty blows. He knew that, though they were necessary to shape a good blade, too many would spoil it.

So, after a while, he would step forward and hold up his hand. " That's enough, now, Sandy," he'd say—and with his own, skilful hands he would finally fashion the blade.

Well, that blacksmith's boy is now a minister. Always, when he hears that tragedy has afflicted one of his flock, his mind goes back to the smiddy where he worked as a boy. For he believes that the heavy blows we suffer in life can shape us into finer, kinder, and more sympathetic folk—just as the blacksmith's hammer shapes the shining blade of the plough.

SUNDAY—JUNE 22.

FORGIVE us our debts, as we forgive our debtors.

MONDAY—JUNE 23.

WHEN Irish friends are about to part they sometimes recite this very old verse:—
May the road rise up to meet you.
May the wind be always at your back.
May the sunshine warm your face
And the rain fall soft on your fields.
And when at last we meet again
May God hold you in the palm of His hand.

THE FRIENDSHIP BOOK

IN 1935 a young man became minister of Glasgow Cathedral.

His name was Nevile Davidson, and perhaps there were some who wondered at one so young holding such a demanding and difficult job.

But the doubters were answered in an unusual way. Not long after he went to Glasgow, the young minister happened to be visiting Loch Lomond. As he stood on the banks, a little girl came rushing up, crying that her Scottie dog was drowning—and sure enough, when he looked, he saw the dog struggling in the loch, twenty yards from the shore.

Without hesitation, he dived into the water, fully clad, and struck out towards the dog. At first it seemed he was too late, for a swift current threatened to drag the Scottie down. But he managed to reach it in time and brought it safely back to the girl.

What has saving a child's dog to do with doing a good job as a minister ?

Some would say, nothing at all. But I disagree; for to me it shows a man of compassion and courage, one who will risk all when duty calls, without counting the cost.

That young minister, who was to hold the highest office in his Church, Moderator of the General Assembly, has now retired from Glasgow Cathedral after 32 splendid years.

WEDNESDAY—JUNE 25.

WHEN unkind things that are not true
  Behind your back are said,
Don't whine or curse and make things worse,
  But, holding high your head,
Just go your own sweet, smiling way—
That's how you're sure to win the day.

THURSDAY—JUNE 26.

IT is a wonderful thing to be clever. It is even more wonderful to be clever and kind.

I am thinking of a small boy who went into hospital to have his tonsils out.

He had never been away from home before, and felt terribly lonely and very much afraid. His one bit of comfort was the teddy bear he hugged, old and battered and with only one eye.

He was still holding the teddy bear when he was wheeled into the operating theatre. As the surgeon approached, a nurse put out her hand to take away the teddy bear. But the surgeon, with a wink at her and at the anaesthetist, murmured— " We'll leave teddy where he is. I think he needs a little attention, too."

When the wee patient came to, teddy was still in his arms, a bandage over its forehead—and two eyes instead of only one.

FRIDAY—JUNE 27.

A GENIAL friend of mine, who ought to have sense enough to make haste slowly, tells me that he boarded a bus a few days ago. He had to run to catch it, and by the time he sat down he was mopping the perspiration from his forehead.

It was only then that he caught sight of a small boy, perhaps four years old, standing on the seat behind, being protected by his mother's arms. The boy had been looking out of the window, but suddenly his interest switched to my friend, whom he surveyed with exceptional interest and obviously deep concern.

At last he leaned forward, and in the gentlest tones said, " There, there, sonny. Don't cry any more. Tell Mummy all about it !"

THE FRIENDSHIP BOOK

I DON'T want to appear too pious, and I am not
wishful to suggest that we should all suddenly
become much more religious than we are. Nevertheless, as I look back at some of the grand stalwarts
of the Church I have known and to the days when
the influence of the Church was greater than it is
now, I find a mighty challenge in the words of
Father Payton, a noted Roman Catholic. Some
years ago he said this to his congregation:—

The family that prays together stays together.

And in my own experience, I can truly say that
—with exceptions here and there—this is pro-
foundly true.

OF the increase of His government and peace
there shall be no end.

NEW to the job, it's not so long since Marion
Harrison took on the job of being post-
mistress to the village. People will come knocking
at her door any hour of the night or day. The fact
that it is supposed to be " half-day " doesn't make
the slightest difference if Marion Harrison is at
home. Still they come, asking for their pensions,
or maybe just for a packet of tea and a chat.

Fortunately, Marion loves her new job, although
nobody would do it for a profit if they took into
account all the long hours that the shop must
be opened, or all the emergency calls—at week-
ends, too. But I think that Marion loves people.
She likes helping people, and this, more than anything, is her reward.

JULY

Tuesday—July 1.

A FRIEND spent a few weeks at the seaside. On a lovely, warm Sunday she went into town to see her husband off on the train back home. She herself was staying on a little longer. When she caught her bus back to the seaside she found herself sitting beside another woman.

It turned out this woman was having a day out — and what a wonderful day it was. For it was the first time she had been out on her own for 20 years! She had been blind all that time—but now the surgeons had restored her sight in one eye.

She knew the other eye would be permanently blind, but, even so, she could see to do the things she'd almost forgotten about. She could read the papers, she could go down town for the messages, she could look into shop windows, and read her own letters. Best of all, she could see again the faces of her family and friends.

Now, on this beautiful summer's day, she was on her way to the seaside, her very first outing by herself, to gaze at the blue sea and sky, at the golden sands, at the children playing on the beach— indeed, to learn again the wonder of what so many of us take for granted.

Doesn't it make your heart warm — and humble?

Wednesday—July 2.

W HEN summer gardens smile she likes
To roam the avenues,
Enjoying other people's scents
And countless rainbow hues.
It's nice to see the flowers sweet
If there's no garden in YOUR street.

THURSDAY—JULY 3.

IT depends on how you read it.

When you have read it, and thought about it a minute, I hope you know which interpretation applies to you. For you are either selfish or un-selfish, kind or not so kind, ready to lend a hand or just a little slow in seeing the need to do so.

The sentence I am thinking of is not as simple as it looks. It was sent to me by a hospital patient, and it reads—*When it comes to doing something for somebody, some folk stop at nothing.*

FRIDAY—JULY 4.

THE Lady of the House and I were visiting Deeside and we set out early one Sunday morning to walk through the woods.

As we approached a clearing, we heard the voices of boys singing " The Lord's My Shepherd," to " Crimond "—and, peeping through the trees, we found a Boys' Brigade company holding an open-air service in front of their camp.

Somehow, on that glorious summer morning amid the stillness and beauty of Deeside, " Crimond " seemed so fitting. It is the first psalm we learn as children. It is the psalm which, more than any other, is chosen for weddings. And it's the psalm which brings comfort to so many as death draws near, and which strengthens those who are left.

Strangely, no one knows for sure who gave us " Crimond." Some say it was Jessie Irvine, daughter of the minister of the parish of Crimond. Others claim the composer was David Grant, an Aberdeen tobacconist.

Does it really matter, I wonder ? For " Crimond " is enshrined in our hearts and heritage.

SATURDAY—JULY 5.

A LONG, rambling letter I received the other day reminded me that somebody once asked President Woodrow Wilson how long it would take him to prepare a ten-minute speech. The President replied, " Two weeks."

" How long," inquired his friend, " would it take to prepare a two-hour speech ?"

" I'm ready now," snapped Woodrow Wilson.

All of which goes to show that the art of speaking or writing is not in how to say a lot, but how to say a lot in a few words.

SUNDAY—JULY 6.

A S one whom his mother comforteth, so will I comfort you.

MONDAY—JULY 7.

THE Salvation Army girl was shocked. She had knocked at the door of a house and the little, bent old lady who opened the door beamed on her visitor. " We want you to come to our services at the Citadel," said the girl. " If you do you will be welcome, and you will get to know Jesus."

" Thank you, dear," was the reply, " that's very nice of you, and from such a bonnie lass, too. But it's my legs—they won't take me that far ; and, really, I've no need to come to the services, though I'd enjoy the singing. You see, the Lord and I have been pals for donkey's years !"

And how surprised the Salvation Army girl was when, having told the Captain about the familiar way in which the old lady had spoken of the Lord, he, too, beamed on her, saying, " Why, that's exactly what we want, my dear !"

FIRST STEPS

> Although we may not understand
> The wherefore and the why,
> The early steps we take are those
> Which count most, by and by.
> The truths learned at a parent's knee
> Make us the folk we grow to be.

DAVID HOPE

GOOD NEIGHBOURS

Terrace or villa, wherever you live,
There is one blessing money can't give —
Neighbours to send the day joking along,
Folk who'll stand by you when all has gone wrong.

DAVID HOPE

TUESDAY—JULY 8.

MR and Mrs White visited the Ayrshire fishing village of Maidens.

As they strolled along the sea front they saw a happy family party sitting down beside a well-laden cloth for a picnic on the beach—mother and father, children, and granny and grandpa, too. It made such a pretty scene that Mr and Mrs White couldn't help pausing to watch for a moment. As they did so they saw every member of the party bow their heads while the father said grace.

It was, says Mr White, a picture he and his wife will long remember—this fine family sitting in silence round their picnic and giving thanks against the glorious background of the blue sea.

In its own way this story is a challenge to us all.

WEDNESDAY—JULY 9.

*W*HENEVER *life's drudgery's hard,*
   Whether you're woman or man ;
Keep on keeping on
Till troubles are gone . . .
   You can always do more than you can !

THURSDAY—JULY 10.

ONE of the greatest Japanese thinkers, Kagawa, died in 1960. His " Psychology of the Poor " is still of enormous importance, and the influence of his dedicated life will long remain.

I like his reference to Christ in one of his writings. It seems at first to say so little—but when you think about it, it says so much —

I read in a book that a man called Christ went about doing good. It is very disconcerting that I am so easily satisfied with just going about.

FRIDAY—JULY 11.

I READ the other day about one of the most distinguished Roman consuls of all time, namely Dentatus, who flourished in the 3rd century B.C., and a man whose name was on everybody's lips. He gained notable victories over the warlike Samnites and Sabines. He led his soldiers to a mighty victory at Beneventum in the year 275 B.C.

Honours were piled upon him. He was hailed as the people's saviour.

Did he let them crown him or reward him with immense riches or embarrass him with a great palace and a thousand servants? Not he. He scorned tributes; and while the going was good, and before somebody (envious of his power) stabbed him in the back, he retired to his own small farm, and spent his days looking after it.

Surely almost-unknown Dentatus deserves to be ranked as one of the wisest men of all?

SATURDAY—JULY 12.

MY knowledge of mathematics is deplorably small. I know that $2 \times 3 = 6$, but not much more. I think I am right in saying that the area of a rectangle is $a \times b$, where a is the length and b the breadth. But Professor Einstein knew a great deal more than that, and was expert in inventing new formulæ.

I understand that he even invented a formula for success in business, and explained to a friend that if a is success, then $a = x + y + z$, where x is work and y is imagination.

His friend nodded. " H'm," said he. " And what does z stand for ?"

Replied Einstein, his eyes twinkling, " Keeping your mouth shut."

THE FRIENDSHIP BOOK

SUNDAY—JULY 13.

WHOSOEVER shall compel thee to go a mile, go with him twain.

MONDAY—JULY 14.

REARED in the old school, Jessie (a widow) has a habit of adding the phrase " If I'm spared," to every sentence concerned even with the simplest future planning. " See you at church on Sunday," she says, " if I'm spared."

One bright afternoon we took a shortcut through the churchyard, where we paused for a minute beside her late husband's grave. Beside the neat headstone lay some fresh-cut flowers. Seeing my interest and sympathy she explained, " That's where he's lain at rest these past sixteen years . . . and there beside him I'll lie some day myself." And then, from habit, she added, " If I'm spared."

TUESDAY—JULY 15.

I HAD been travelling by train and when I reached the ticket barrier there was a woman in front of me. Now, while madam was searching for her ticket, she dropped her purse.

Gallantly, I bent down—as any man would— to retrieve it for her. And, bless my soul, as I reached out for it, her foot came down on it— quick as a flash. Swiftly she stooped and picked up the purse, with a curious glance at me.

I straightened, smiled, and explained I was trying to help. She just mumbled and passed through the barrier.

I don't know why, friends, but I felt a bit sad . . . maybe because in these days an act of common courtesy could be mistaken for something else.

WEDNESDAY—JULY 16.

THEY walked together, hand in hand,
In sunshine after rain,
Along the street, he dark, she fair—
I smiled to see the twain.
And how or why I can't explain,
But I, now old, felt young again.

THURSDAY—JULY 17.

THIS is a remarkable story of a remarkable man.

Every week Jimmy Hamilton travels at least 200 miles to visit a thousand patients in hospitals as far apart as Glasgow, Kirkcaldy and Bridge of Earn. Yet the astonishing thing is that for over fifty years Jimmy has been without legs, ever since he was in a railway accident as a boy of three.

Jimmy's unique mission began many years ago when he visited a hospital near his home and realised for the first time how lonely some patients can be. He vowed he would do all he could for them, even though he was badly handicapped.

So he began travelling by bus to hospitals around Motherwell, found which patients needed cheering up most, and sat by their beds until he made them smile. As the years passed, more and more patients blessed him for what he did.

Indeed, so grateful were they that they and their relatives presented him with a car so he could go even farther afield—and now he visits no fewer than nine hospitals every week, paying all his expenses himself. Often surgeons send for him to give their patients new hope.

It's easy to find an excuse for not doing a job, especially when you're as handicapped as he is. So I say, "Bravo, Jimmy," for proving so magnificently that where there's a will, there's always a way.

FRIDAY—JULY 18.

GEORDIE HAMILTON'S fish and chip shop was well known ; and even when Geordie was going on for 80 he still retained his love of wild flowers and of garden flowers, too.

I think, however, older folk will remember Geordie best and longest for what he did in middle life. In those days he went around the district with a buggy drawn by a pony, and he did a brisk summer trade in ice cream. As somebody remarked, " Geordie's ice cream went down fine." It tasted all the better because handed out with a smile.

And wherever there was a Sunday School treat in a field, there, sure as eggs are eggs, would be Geordie. A good business move, you might say.

But you would be wrong ! Geordie Hamilton, who loved children even more than flowers, was not selling ice cream. He was giving it away !

SATURDAY—JULY 19.

ROBERT and Jill were travelling by bus when the following brief conversation ensued between brother and sister—Robert, wise and experienced at 11, Jill, eager and inquisitive at 9 :

" What's that, Robert ?"

" That is an observatory."

" What's an observatory ?"

" That," said Robert gently but firmly, " is your assignment for today."

Jill did not pout. She smiled happily; and the minute she was home she took down an encyclopædia, and read all about observatories.

You may think it all a bit odd, but nobody can know too much these days. Moreover, finding out is a great game—and what you discover for yourself you tend to remember.

SUNDAY—JULY 20.

BLESSED are the merciful : for they shall obtain mercy.

MONDAY—JULY 21.

ONE of the most learned and gracious women of last century was Anna Letitia Barbauld, who died in 1825. She lived graciously and died almost with a song on her lips, because the last time she put pen to paper she wrote these glorious and challenging lines :

Life, we have been long together
Through pleasant and through cloudy weather.
  'Tis hard to part when friends are dear—
  Perhaps 'twill cost a sigh, a tear.
Then steal away, give little warning,
    Choose thine own time.
   Say not, " Good night," but in some brighter clime
     Bid me, " Good morning !"

TUESDAY—JULY 22.

TWO patients in the surgical ward of a hospital were having a heart-to-heart talk recently. They lay in adjacent beds, and both men were getting on in years, both finding it a bit difficult to feel comfortable and confident after their operations.

" Jim," said one to the other when they were both feeling a bit doubtful of their chances of ever returning home, " we've just got to keep on doing as we're told and waiting to see how things work out. After all, where there's life there's hope."

" Andy," replied the other, " you're very nearly right, but you're just slightly off the beam. What you really mean is, where there's hope there's life."

THE FRIENDSHIP BOOK

WEDNESDAY—JULY 23.

*L*IFE'S *often cruel : undeserved,*
Some sudden knock-out blow
Which staggers us, we reel, we fall—
The beating lays us low.
How sad. But splendid if, with pain,
We slowly rise, and smile again !

THURSDAY—JULY 24.

YOU don't believe in miracles ? Then let me tell you about Patrick Francis Dominic Muldoon.

At 21, when most sons step into manhood, Paddy chose to become an outcast. He fought and drank and stole. From a fine lad with a steady job, he sank so low the law forbade him to enter his own home because of the distress he caused.

Hardly a year went by without him being sent to prison. Such was life for Paddy for 16 years.

One winter he slept in bushes near a men's hostel. The Salvation Army officer in charge of the hostel found him there, took compassion on him, encouraged him, and gave him work as a porter.

Then the miracle happened. A few months later Paddy went to a little service in the hostel. He hardly knew why, for religion hadn't interested him before. Yet, when men were asked to come forward if they wanted to start a new life, Paddy walked forward, went down on his knees and wept as he said he wanted to make a fresh start.

The amazing thing is, Paddy Muldoon was changed beyond belief from that moment. He has become a member of the Salvation Army. He is reunited with his family. You won't find a happier man anywhere.

Doesn't it show, my friend, that however black the night, there can always be a new dawn ?

FRIDAY—JULY 25.

THE minister had had a grand holiday with plenty of sunshine.

Yes, he thought, but what about the old and sick who aren't well enough to go on holiday? Well, he decided, the next best thing to having a holiday yourself is to share someone else's!

So, that Sunday, he drew up a list of all the housebound folk in his congregation and announced that if anyone cared to send them a card it would fill their room with sunshine.

The result is that every year 20 or 30 postcards find their way into the homes of the pensioners, often from folk they don't even know, whisking them off in their imagination to places like Italy, Switzerland, Majorca, even Canada and America.

SATURDAY—JULY 26.

A GOLDEN wedding anniversary is quite an event, but James and Mary are so shy that nobody would have known but for Mrs Grey. But she couldn't make a splash because James and Mary wouldn't have liked it.

So she got busy. She arranged on that day for the gallant couple to be dressed in their best. She persuaded them to sit by the living-room window. Since you can hardly have an unveiling ceremony without an audience, she asked Mr Whittington and Miss Dumble to be present. She herself, at the chosen moment, made a speech to wish James and Mary all the best, and then pulled aside the curtains to reveal a new bird table, the two visitors clapping . . . and then all had tea and cake.

" They were like little children," said Mrs Grey. " So pleased, so thrilled . . . and so glad there wasn't a fuss."

THE INTRUDER

Across our skies the stranger flew.
The air re-echoed to his roar.
Then he was gone and watchers knew
A silence deeper than before.

DAVID HOPE

LEGS BEFORE WHEELS

Walk up, walk up, here's your chance,
The donkeys are ready to go ;
Neddy will trot and Dot may prance,
And Tom ? — well, you never do know !

Hurry along, there's a steed for each,
They all love earning their meals;
Fashions may change, but down on the beach
Legs are still better than wheels.

DAVID HOPE

THE BOSS

When people say a dog I own,
I courteously agree :
But if the truth were only known —
My dog owns me!

DAVID HOPE

SUNDAY—JULY 27.

WHAT doth the Lord require of thee, but to do justly, and to love mercy, and to walk humbly with thy God?

MONDAY—JULY 28.

LORD REITH, speaking to the students at his installation as Lord Rector of Glasgow University, said this:—

" I can only tell you what I believe and what I hope you will find : that religion, or some definite commanding confession, Christian or otherwise, is an integral part of life ; the supreme factor for service and success and happiness."

Look around you, at those who have achieved something worthwhile, whether they be great figures in public life or ordinary people living a quiet existence, and I am sure you will see that Lord Reith's statement is a true one.

TUESDAY—JULY 29.

I SHALL not readily forget these words of Professor William Barclay —

It is hunger which gives food its taste.

It is thirst which makes cool, clear water taste like nectar.

It is tiredness which makes sleep a boon.

It is toil which makes rest a blessing.

It is loneliness which gives friendship its value.

It is the rain which gives sunshine its joy.

It is the dark night which gives the dawn its glory.

It is parting which makes meeting again a happy thing . . .

WEDNESDAY—JULY 30.

Y ES, little feet come running fast
When little knees are sore;
How gently Mum wipes little tears
Till all is well once more.
It's helping precious children smile
That makes a mother's day worthwhile.

THURSDAY—JULY 31.

A BABY had just been born to a young wife of
barely 20. It was her first child, but alas, it
soon became clear that the baby, a little girl, would
not live more than a few hours. It was a bitter blow,
but the young couple both wanted one thing—that
their child should be christened.

So, late as it was, the Rev. Alex. Farrow drove to
the Infirmary. There he was led to the room where
the baby lay. Before he could enter, he had to slip
on a white mask, cap and robe, and scrub his hands
as thoroughly as a surgeon.

Only then could the simple ceremony begin—
and how different it was from the usual christening
service. There were no flowers, no font, no baptismal
hymn. Only Mr Farrow and a staff nurse were there,
standing beside the incubator.

Quietly, the minister offered up a short prayer.
Then, pushing a teaspoon of water through a gap in
the incubator, he gently sprinkled a little on the
baby's brow and spoke her name, Sharon. Somehow, the blessing as the service ended had never
sounded so poignant . . . " The Lord lift up His
countenance upon thee, and give thee peace . . ."

Not long afterwards, Sharon died. But I know
that, in their sorrow, her father and mother will be
comforted by the thought of that service in a little
room in the Infirmary.

AUGUST

FRIDAY—AUGUST 1.

SOME years ago Clara Simpson was deeply moved by a story she had read—the story of a man who had lost his wife, and found the lonely road before him hard to travel. Somehow, as she read the story, she realised her own loneliness and her need of a faith to help her to keep on; and out of that emotional crisis came a poem which has blessed many, especially those who are nearing life's sunset. One verse of her poem means much to me:—

> Strengthen my heart for the journey,
>   Strong may I be to the end,
> Knowing that Thou art beside me,
>   Saviour, Redeemer and Friend.
> Leading me onward and upward
>   Where the dear loved ones I'll see,
> Strengthen my heart for the journey
>   Unto eternity.

SATURDAY—AUGUST 2.

ODD that people often say what they don't mean. One of the best examples of this is the sentence known to every schoolboy: When a Frenchman in England fell into a river, he threw up his arms and yelled, " I will drown and nobody shall save me."

A more recent example which has come to my notice is a traffic regulation issued by U.S. police forces. They are experts at keeping the traffic flowing; but I think somebody slipped up badly when he drew up the following rule: " When two motor vehicles meet at an intersection, each shall come to a full stop, and neither shall proceed till the other has gone."

THE FRIENDSHIP BOOK

IN quietness and in confidence shall be your strength.

I DON'T know who first wrote these rather quaint and old-fashioned lines, but I think young parents today may well take them to heart—

Before your child has come to seven,
Teach him well the way to heaven.
Better still the truth will thrive,
If he knows it when he's five.
Best of all if, at your knee,
He learns it when he's only three.

FOR some years Mrs McLennan was a district nurse on the Isle of Skye.

She made many friends there, and met many fine folk. And she told a friend of mine a rather remarkable thing about Skye.

In almost every home she visited, she found the old granny or grandpa sitting in a chair by the side of the fire, an honoured member of the family. It seems that the people of Skye still firmly believe that the right place for an old mother and father to be is with their own folk. When they are no longer able to live in their own homes and look after themselves, their sons and daughters regard it not just a duty but a privilege to welcome them.

Indeed, Mrs McLennan went on to say that in Skye there is a lovely eventide home with empty places in it—simply because so many old people are living happily in their own family circle.

How delighted I am to hear it.

WEDNESDAY—AUGUST 6.

R EMEMBER, please, all tired folk—
No holiday have they;
Policemen, nurses, waitresses,
Who must keep on all day.
If now you rest, remember such . . .
You need their help so very much.

THURSDAY—AUGUST 7.

MRS MOORE recently had the good fortune to be in hospital.

Good fortune, you ask? Well, they're Mrs Moore's own words, for she lives alone, and finds loneliness hard to bear sometimes. But in hospital she was surrounded by friendly folk — and, even though she'd no one to visit her, she looked forward to the visiting hour. For many visitors brought their children with them, so daintily dressed—as Mrs Moore says, just like rays of sunshine.

One day, a wee girl who'd come to see her granny, trotted over to Mrs Moore's bed. " Why have you no visitors ?" she demanded. The old lady explained gently she'd nobody who could come. " What's your name ?" the child asked. Mrs Moore smiled. " Muriel," she replied.

The little girl's eyes sparkled. " That's a pretty name," she said. " I'll visit you each time I come to see Granny, and when I'm saying my prayers I'll ask Jesus to keep Muriel from feeling lonely, and help her to get better. He'll know who I mean." And with another smile, she was off.

Now Mrs Moore is home again—but when she's feeling lonely, she pictures a little girl kneeling at her bed at night, solemnly asking help for an old lady who's all alone. That picture does more to dispel her loneliness than words can ever say.

FRIDAY—AUGUST 8.

THESE lines were passed on to me by an old minister, who found them a comfort through all his many years of service:

Whenever I am troubled and lost in deep despair, I bundle all my worries up, and go to God in prayer. I tell Him I am sick at heart, and lost and lonely, too, that my mind is deeply burdened, and I don't know what to do.

But I know He stilled the tempest, and calmed the angry sea, and I humbly ask if, in His love, He'll do the same for me. And then I just keep quiet, and think only thoughts of peace, and in the shadow of His arm my anxious cares shall cease.

SATURDAY—AUGUST 9.

MRS HOUSTON went to Argyll with her husband and three boys. On a perfect summer day they were all climbing in Glencoe when Mrs Houston fell and broke her ankle badly.

She was taken to hospital, and was told she'd be there for three weeks. " What a way to spend a holiday," she thought ruefully. " Imagine being stuck in a hospital ward."

But the more she thought about it, the more she realised she was, in fact, having the kind of holiday she'd often dreamed about. She could look forward to three weeks of absolute rest, with no dishes to wash, no meals to prepare, no housework to do, and no lively laddies to keep an eye on. Instead, she'd be waited on hand and foot, while her family were coping on their own, learning to be independent and helpful !

A complete change from the daily routine and a rare tonic for weary feet and a tired back. What more, asks Mrs Houston, could a woman wish for ?

THE FRIENDSHIP BOOK

SUNDAY—AUGUST 10.

FEAR God, and keep His commandments : for this is the whole duty of man.

MONDAY—AUGUST 11.

THIS recipe must surely appeal to every mother !
Take half a dozen children, two small dogs, a pinch of clear, rippling stream and some pebbles.

Put the ingredients in a large, grassy field, stirring constantly. Pour the brook over the pebbles, sprinkle the field with flowers, spread a deep-blue sky over all and bake in a hot sun.

When the children are well browned, remove and set to cool in a bathtub !

TUESDAY—AUGUST 12.

MR McPHERSON TOUGH is the chemist, newsagent and bookseller in the Argyllshire village of Inveraray.

Outside his shop are rows of postcards, newspapers, comics and paper-back books. In the window of the shop is a notice—" WHEN SHOP IS CLOSED, PLEASE HELP YOURSELF AND PLACE MONEY THROUGH LETTER-BOX."

Perfectly reasonable, I'd say, so far as papers, postcards and comics are concerned. But when it comes to leaving a pile of books outside . . . well, there are those who might find themselves tempted.

Yet, though the books lie there with nobody about to keep an eye on things, the trusting shopkeeper of Inveraray is scarcely ever let down. Even when he is, it makes no difference to him. " It's their conscience," he says with a smile, " not mine !"

If we trusted more readily, we, too, might find that human nature isn't as bad as it's made out to be.

WEDNESDAY—AUGUST 13.

LAUGH as you may, I want to say
  That saints and angels shine
In this dark world, and heroes too,
Whose gracious lives touch mine.
These splendid ones you, too, can meet —
If you expect to — in the street.

THURSDAY—AUGUST 14.

I WOULD like to pay tribute to a farmer called John Brown, who died over 30 years ago.

With his father and mother, he came to the farm of Peasiehill on the edge of Arbroath when he was a lad of eight, and it was his home for the rest of his life. He might have passed his years there quietly, sowing and harvesting, raising his cattle and sheep, just as his father had done.

But John was aye looking for a way to improve things, and for years he had patiently tried to produce a new potato. Time and again he planted his seeds and carefully examined the results—but, always, he put them aside. For he demanded perfection, and he was prepared to wait all his days to get it.

Then one morning he lifted from the rich brown earth a potato that made all his years of hard work worth while. It was a big, new, wholesome, golden potato that surpassed anything he had ever seen before. As he turned it over in his hands his eyes shone with pride. " Ay," he murmured softly, " ye're a golden wonder !"

That, my friend, is how the Golden Wonder potato came to be—and all of us who believe, as I do, that a dish of tasty, floury potatoes takes a lot of beating, should remember the old Arbroath farmer who wasn't content with second best.

THE ABBEY STEPS

The monks arc dust,
Yet, passing by,
Their presence still I know;
These men who sought
The same as I—
My brothers long ago!

DAVID HOPE

SEA MUSIC

The folks who live along the shore
  Have music all day long,
And all night through as well they hear
  The sea's eternal song.

DAVID HOPE

THE FRIENDSHIP BOOK

LONG ago somebody said there were two kinds of people. How right he was.

Since time immemorial there have been rich and poor, good and bad, old and young, and so on. But the wise man whose words I quote said—*There are two kinds of people: those who wear badly and those who wear well.*

The folk who wear badly usually begin by making a good impression . . . they are so pleasant, ready to flatter, and so eager to help. But as time goes on you find them just not as wonderful as you were sure they were at first.

The second type are folk who, at first, are perhaps a bit too quiet, anything but fascinating or amusing and certainly never showy . . . but as time goes on you discover they mean what they say, they lend a hand, and you can depend upon them. The first wear badly. The others wear well.

To which group would you prefer to belong?

A LITTLE while ago I heard about Gene Hatton, an ex-prisoner of war who has been in Deva Hospital, Cheshire, for many years.

I sent him a few flowers.

But that was nothing compared with what Gene sent me. It was a scrap of paper, something I shall always treasure, for it was written by a hero who has suffered much yet never complains.

On it were written six words which, because of his infirmity, took him 25 minutes to write—25 minutes of supreme effort and determination. The six words were—" Francis Gay thank you Gene Hatton."

That is all but that is everything.

SUNDAY—AUGUST 17.

THEY that are whole need not a physician; but they that are sick.

MONDAY—AUGUST 18.

IT is good to hear of someone, busy and important, taking time and trouble to reassure an elderly person at a time when such help is most needed.

Doris Angelina (we always give her the full name) is nearly 70. Soon she must go into hospital to undergo an operation for cataract in one eye.

" Can I have a couple of days' notice, please, before I come in ?" she asked the consultant. " I would like a little time to get everything into order."

" We'll surely manage to give you more notice than that," said the surgeon.

Only a few words, but how reassuring.

TUESDAY—AUGUST 19.

EVER wondered why a church has a spire? At one time, of course, a tower made a good lookout when danger threatened. Also by raising a tower above the roofs of the houses people could see the time on the clock; and long before the days of clocks, towers housed the bells which summoned folk to worship or tolled for the dead.

But I think the fundamental reason was that the church spire lifted men's eyes above the things of time to the changing but infinite sky.

" Look up !" said the spire of the old church. " Look up. There is more in life than today, more than work and money and fashion and bickering and scandal . . . there are the timeless things of God. Look up, and let your soul grow big."

So men built their churches with spires.

THE FRIENDSHIP BOOK

HOW very nice it is to meet
A person who can smile;
Somehow it helps to keep life sweet
And cheer us up a while.
If someone's smile can help you through,
Please smile at folk when they meet you!

THURSDAY—AUGUST 21.

MR WILLIAM WILSON is an Edinburgh artist, who, for many years, has spent all his time creating magnificent stained glass windows. You will find his work in the cathedrals of Canterbury, Liverpool, Glasgow, St Giles' and Brechin, in St Machar's in Aberdeen, and many more too numerous to mention.

Yet, even as he was working on these beautiful windows, his sight was failing, and a few years ago he went completely blind. A tragedy for anyone, but for an artist, how much more so.

But he is still creating his stained glass windows, even in his blindness, and those who are best able to judge say they surpass all that he has done before. As I write, he is busy on windows for churches in Britain and America.

How does he do it? In some unique way, he is able to plan in his mind how he wants the finished window to look. He forms the design and chooses the colours, then carefully passes on his directions to his assistants. And the astonishing thing is that, though he never sees the windows he creates, each is a masterpiece, exactly as he imagined it.

It is surely a humbling thought to us all that one who is blind can see such wondrous colours, and can use them to bring even more beauty to the loveliest buildings in the land.

JOHN MASEFIELD, Poet Laureate, has gone to his last rest, but much that he wrote will endure for a long, long time.

Two of his lines—not, perhaps, the most famous of his lines—live with me.

I have seen flowers in stony places.
And kindness done by men with ugly faces.

I, too, have seen such things. I remember a mother in a slum over twenty years ago—the face of a Madonna as she nursed a sick child, crooning over it in a shaft of evening sunlight.

I have seen kindness done by unlovely people— a hungry lorry driver, unshaved for 36 hours, uncouth, roughly-spoken, slipping a hot meat pie into the hands of a tramp.

The amazing fact is that in a world where so much is deplorable there is so much that is fine and clean and heart-warming and truly magnificent.

ROBERT, aged three, is the proud possessor of a diminutive tricycle. He sits on that tricycle hour after hour. He rides round the garden on it. Every day when his sister, Marjorie, comes home from school (she is practically grown up, being five and a bit) Robert goes to meet her on his tricycle.

One day Marjorie said: " Robert, if you spend your life on that tricycle your legs will go rusty."

That bothered Robert a wee bit. But not enough to make him walk. He still went along the pavement to meet Marjorie coming home from school . . . but every now and then he nipped off his tricycle, took an anxious look at his little fat legs, and gently fingered them to make quite sure they were not getting rusty !

THE FRIENDSHIP BOOK

SUNDAY—AUGUST 24.

THE labourer is worthy of his hire.

MONDAY—AUGUST 25.

JEAN lives a happy life in spite of lots of troubles—
a large family, an ailing mother and the worry
of wondering whether her husband will be made
redundant soon.

Her secret is simple. She says her prayers, and
does as much as she can for everybody round about.
And whenever she feels like sitting down and
worrying, she glances at a little card above the
kitchen sink—and up goes her chin. It says: *Anybody
who just drifts with the current is sure to end up in
deep water.*

TUESDAY—AUGUST 26.

THE giant jet flew towards the setting sun at more
than 500 m.p.h. We had just seen Mrs Collie
off at the airport. She was going to visit her daughter
whom she hadn't seen in ten years. All expenses
were being paid from the other side. The odd thing
would be that, when she landed at New York in
six or seven hours, it would still be daylight.

Nowadays life moves much more quickly than
it has ever done; speed is of the essence. Time-
saving gadgets grow more necessary every day—
whether they be food mixers, computers or the latest
jet planes. And what do we do with the time and
energy we save? We can spend it in gay living, or
searching for ways of making more and more money.
Or we can spend it—or at least some of it—in helping
others less fortunate than ourselves, and trying to
live a better life.

The choice is ours.

WEDNESDAY—AUGUST 27.

*T*HE *August sun for most is fun—*
We laze around or play;
But summer heat has old folk beat—
They're short of breath, they say.
It's nice to lend such folk a hand,
So we can show we understand.

THURSDAY—AUGUST 28.

THE minister in a Methodist church, announcing the first hymn, said, "Our worship will commence with hymn No. 246." But before he could say another word a young man stood up in the centre of the church. "Why?" he asked.

The congregation simply couldn't believe their ears. Heads turned, eyebrows rose—and the laddie's mother thought she was going to faint.

But the minister wasn't perturbed. "Well now," he smiled, "that's a good question. Just why do we sing hymns?" And he proceeded to explain.

A few minutes later, as the minister prepared to read the Old Testament lesson, a second young person stood up before the astonished congregation. What on earth, he asked, has the Old Testament to do with modern life? Again the minister answered.

Altogether four young folk stood up during the service and challenged the minister, demanding to know why we should sing, read from the Bible, pray, &c. And, though the congregation didn't know it, it was all planned by the minister and youth fellowship beforehand, designed to make folk sit up and think about what they were doing.

I'm sure you don't need me to tell you it did just that—or that it was one of the most successful services ever.

THE FRIENDSHIP BOOK

FRIDAY—AUGUST 29.

ARE you missing something important?
I ask this question because of a little story I heard the other day—a tale told by Mr Parry. Time and time again, it seems, he had driven by a wood outside Stratford-on-Avon, taking no notice of it, hearing and seeing nothing of interest. One summer evening, a friend suggested they should pull up at the roadside. They did so, and Mr Parry sat listening. A moment or two later the intense silence was broken by the sound of exquisite bird-music—a nightingale was singing so wonderfully that both listeners were captivated.

It makes you think, doesn't it? So easy to be too quick, too noisy and too pre-occupied—too busy to hear or see the things that enrich life most.

SATURDAY—AUGUST 30.

LANG WILLIE was a caddie at St Andrews. One day, a long time ago, he found himself teaching a professor from the university the rudiments of the noble game.

Unfortunately, the professor made only a very poor showing with his clubs. Unfortunately, also, Lang Willie had never been blessed with a great deal of patience. At last he exploded, uttering what have since become famous words—" Ye see, Professor, as long as ye're learning the lads at the college Latin and Greek, it's easy work, but when ye come to play golf ye must hae a heid !"

SUNDAY—AUGUST 31.

JOY shall be in heaven over one sinner that repenteth, more than over ninety and nine just persons, which need no repentance.

SEPTEMBER

SAM MARX, of film fame, once tried to make a collection of four-word sentences into which a lot of wisdom can be packed. For example, among his compact bits of wisdom are such truths as:

> Let sleeping dogs lie.
> In God we trust.
> Live and let live.
> Charity begins at home.
> This, too, shall pass.

I confess this hobby intrigued me, and I found myself thinking up four-word aphorisms by the dozen. I am tempted to share them with you; but on second thoughts I feel sure you will be happier if you think them up for yourselves.

A worthwhile game, don't you think?

IF you ask me, no one enjoys poking fun at ministers more than ministers themselves!

Like this tale told to me by one of them.

It was a glorious Sunday morning, but the minister in the pulpit, who was on holiday relief, was oblivious to the sunshine, the blue skies, and sparkling sea outside. On and on went his sermon until, at last, he brought his oration to an end.

" I'm sorry if I got carried away," he told the beadle later in the vestry when he saw that worthy glancing at his watch. " The text just held me and I couldn't let go. I hope the congregation won't resent being kept so long."

" Don't worry yourself, minister," replied the beadle. " After all, you've fairly shortened the year for them!"

WEDNESDAY—SEPTEMBER 3.

> *Y*OU *can't make speeches ? Star in films ?*
>   *A poet you're simply not ?*
> *If many things you cannot do,*
>   *I wouldn't grieve a lot.*
> *Maybe you're born to ease the load*
>   *Of some old person down the road ?*

THURSDAY—SEPTEMBER 4.

BERT COWIE was a coalman.

In the old days he used to drive his horse and cart round the quiet roads of Kincardineshire.

Always, he was a welcome visitor, and I know there were occasions when, if a family had fallen on hard times, an extra bag mysteriously found its way into the cellar—with no mention of payment, of course.

As the years passed, Bert's horse and cart gave way to a motor lorry. But Bert himself was always the same, a friendly man doing a humble job and delighting in doing it well.

During the last few months he was on the road, he would stop at the gate of the church when he had finished his rounds, walk up the path, and peep inside. For, under his leadership, it was being restored, and his day was not complete unless he paused to see that all was well.

It was a proud day for him when the church was dedicated anew—but it was a sad day for his friends who crowded into the same church not very long after to pay tribute to his memory, for Bert had died quite suddenly.

If you look at Bert's gravestone, you won't see written upon it—" He was a coalman to the glory of God," but the words are true all the same, and I cannot think of a more noble epitaph.

FRIDAY—SEPTEMBER 5.

IF you think of harvest thanksgiving simply in terms of golden sheaves and a table laden with flowers and fruit, you haven't got the true picture.

I'm thinking of something that happened during a service in a Salvation Army citadel.

The children went forward to present their harvest offerings at the front of the hall. Suddenly, there was a pause in the orderly procession. The congregation turned, wondering why it had halted—and then they saw one of the young Salvationists bend forward and lift up a little cripple child in his arms. Gently he carried the boy to the table to hand over his offering.

It was perhaps the most moving moment of the service and no one who was there will forget the look of joy on the child's face.

But more, it reminded them of the harvest of blessings that is reaped by all of us all the year round—the blessings of health and strength, of the helping hand, of courage and cheerfulness when the going's hard, and of the privilege of giving.

SATURDAY—SEPTEMBER 6.

THE student was struggling along the Edinburgh street with what might be an empty soap box in one hand, plus a bundle of papers in the other. He gratefully accepted my offer of a lift, box and all. It appeared that he was going to speak for his political party among all the other week-end orators at the foot of the Mound.

What his party might be, I did not ask. When he left me, I had the feeling that there was not much fear for democracy, so long as such young men were not frightened to speak their minds, nor yet too proud to take a soap box with them.

THE FRIENDSHIP BOOK

SUNDAY—SEPTEMBER 7.

WHILE the earth remaineth, seedtime and harvest, and cold and heat, and summer and winter, and day and night shall not cease.

MONDAY—SEPTEMBER 8.

I CANNOT remember where I first heard this old proverb, but as I look around me at the golden harvest fields, I cannot help thinking how apt it is—

Who learns and learns,
Nor acts on what he knows,
Is one who ploughs and ploughs,
But never sows . . .

TUESDAY—SEPTEMBER 9.

ONE day last century an American woman found herself making bread yet again—making bread in the same old bowl and in the same old way as she had been making it for years. There, alone in her kitchen, she told herself she never wanted to make any more bread as long as she lived.

Then she realised that there was no escaping that chore.

Suddenly a new thought struck her. She paused a moment, and then began humming happily to herself. Later in the day she wrote a letter to her husband telling him: " I've won a victory. It came to me when I was making bread. Here I am, compelled to make it. Why not, I thought, consider making bread a pleasurable occupation, and trying to see how well I can make and bake it ?"

The best thing about this story is that it is true. The letter about bread is still to be seen. The gallant woman who wrote it was the wife of James Abram Garfield, later President of the United States.

WEDNESDAY—SEPTEMBER 10.

WHY not find the time to pray:
    " Bless all needy folk today."
Good to think, where some are sad,
Cheer will come to make them glad.
God a miracle might do:
Cheering folk by sending you!

THURSDAY—SEPTEMBER 11.

A JOINER to trade, Hugh Ingram keeps a small home farm going, mainly to provide milk, butter, and cheese for the old Manor House. Few servants remain. Barbara Ingram, his wife, has a notice " Bed and Breakfast " at the end of the lane. This was how, on a holiday trip, we came to know them.

In the morning we watched him rebuilding the old dairy with skilled hands. I told him: " You could be doing far better for yourself, Mr Ingram, as a maintenance man in one of the big factories." " That's a fact," he answered, taking some nails out of his mouth.

Barbara Ingram went on to explain how, as long as her mother had lived, the folk at the Manor had provided her with a home, free fuel and light, as well as a small pension. " Only the old dowager is left now," she explained, " and we couldn't really leave her. She was so decent to my father before he died, and to my mother for years afterwards, that we will never go as long as she lives."

It is not fashionable to talk about the " good old days " ; but I think they were good sometimes. There was this sense of loyalty between master and man, or between maid and mistress, which is now almost totally lost. We might be none the worse today for some of the old-fashioned virtues.

FRIDAY—SEPTEMBER 12.

THREE-YEAR-OLD Amanda Emms spent two weeks in hospital, and naturally Mrs Emms visited her every day.

The worst part came at the end of the visit. The little girl almost broke her heart, pleading through the sobs for Mummy to stay. Indeed, when Mrs Emms reached home, she couldn't help having a weep herself, at the thought of the wee face streaming with tears.

Then, one night, the dreaded moment arrived again. But this time there were no tears. In fact, Amanda waved cheerily to her Mum, and smiled brightly as she left.

Now I'd have guessed that Mrs Emms would feel happier about that, and that there would be no tears from her that night, either. But there were. More than ever, in fact. For Mrs Emms had convinced herself her wee girl didn't need her any more !

Happily, Amanda is now home, and all's well again. But isn't that the kind of thing that makes mothers mothers ?

SATURDAY—SEPTEMBER 13.

AT the next table in the restaurant the young man was fishing in his pockets. Evidently he could not find what he sought. When the waitress brought the coffee we overheard him ask—" Do you sell cigarettes ?"

The waitress said, " No, I'm sorry." A few minutes later she was back, producing from her apron pocket her own packet and offering a cigarette to the customer.

Cigarette smoking is going out of fashion for health reasons; but as between hardened sinners, it was a charming little touch of courtesy.

SUNDAY—SEPTEMBER 14.

THOU shalt not avenge, nor bear any grudge against the children of thy people, but thou shalt love thy neighbour as thyself.

MONDAY—SEPTEMBER 15.

ABOUT four centuries ago an Italian sculptor set to work to carve a figure out of a huge block of marble. He worked hard and long till one day tragedy occurred. His chisel slipped, a long splinter of marble came away, and the statue was ruined. Defeated and utterly cast down, the sculptor turned aside from his work, and the marble remained untouched year after year — so much waste.

At last another sculptor saw the ruined block, studied it, was caught up by a flashing vision, and with hammer and chisel set to work to carve a figure—the figure of David. What the first artist in stone had regarded as a fault, the second artist in stone—Michelangelo, himself—realised was an opportunity, something which with skill and imagination could be turned to good account.

The worthless block of marble is now one of the most beautiful statues in the world.

TUESDAY—SEPTEMBER 16.

WHAT is an hour compared with a lifetime? A very insignificant part of our span of years. And if an hour is not much, a minute is, surely, a mere trifle; and what is a split second either way?

But half a sixtieth of a minute can make all the difference, as a wise man reminds us in a telling phrase. He was Jean de la Bruyere, who lived in the 17th century; and he said: *There are some people who speak one moment before they think.*

THE FRIENDSHIP BOOK

YOU walked together down the years,
Such hard, sweet years now lost;
Today you walk alone—and smile
But, oh, how great the cost.
Smile as you walk in step with one
You cannot see, but has not gone.

MRS BELLA FRASER is over 70 now, and a charming, silver-haired old lady. But this story begins away back in 1917. In that year, more than 300 young men came to Ross-shire from America to help the First World War effort by working as lumberjacks in the forests around Ardgay.

At the time, Bella worked in the post office there. She grew to know the young Americans, for they came to the post office to collect their letters.

Before they returned to America, they all came to bid her good-bye, and to tell her they'd never forget all she had done. Bella assured them she'd never forget them, either—and she hasn't.

When the men held their first reunion in America in 1920, a parcel arrived for them from Scotland. When they opened it, they found over 300 sprigs of white heather, one for every man there. It had come from Bella.

And every autumn since, when the heather is at its best, Bella takes to the hills and climbs to the secret spots where white heather grows. She fills her basket with sprigs, parcels them up, and sends them off to America in time for the annual reunion of the men who waved good-bye so long ago.

Bella doesn't expect she'll ever see any of them again—yet, so long as they live, they will be linked together in this lovely way.

FRIDAY—SEPTEMBER 19.

MRS BURNETT, who lives near Ballater, is a truly remarkable soul.

For Mrs Burnett has been blind for over 50 years. Yet she lives alone, cooks her meals and does her own housework—even to washing and polishing the windows through which she never sees.

She's full of praise for her neighbours, one of whom looks in every day to read her letters to her.

Yes, there are many kinds of courage, but I often think the noblest kind is that indomitable spark that keeps a man or woman going forward day by day, despite grievous handicaps, and without a murmur of complaint.

SATURDAY—SEPTEMBER 20.

JIMMY BOYD was a Govan fireman, but had to give up his job while still in his fifties, because of illness. He's never been able to work again, and he might well have missed the comradeship of the men he worked with. But no—for the firemen of Govan have kept in touch with Jimmy, visiting him regularly and giving him all their news.

But there's better to come. Not long ago Jimmy and his wife were given a new council house. How thrilled they were as they walked round, planning where all their bits and pieces were to go. Then there was a knock at the door—and who should they find on the step but the Govan Fire Brigade!

No, they hadn't come to put out a fire. Instead of hoses and helmets, they came armed with pots of paint, rolls of paper, brushes, and paste—everything, in fact, that's needed to decorate a house. And, with a smile and a song, they did just that—decorating their friend's house from top to bottom!

No wonder Jimmy's proud of his mates.

BEGINNINGS

The waters as they roar to sea
 A song of triumph sing;
Strange to think great rivers start
 With just a tiny spring.

DAVID HOPE

PATIENCE

You cannot press a switch
And make the wind blow;
Wishing will not make
Time move fast — or slow.
In our many jousts with fate
The lesson we must learn is — wait.   DAVID HOPE

SUNDAY—SEPTEMBER 21.

LAY up for yourselves treasures in heaven.

MONDAY—SEPTEMBER 22.

IT'S almost twenty years since Mrs Black passed away. For the last five years of her life, the old lady lay in bed, unable to turn or raise herself. Yet, each night, she prayed for everyone she knew— family, friends, neighbours, her minister, the doctor —and many others she had heard about. Then, and only then, she would ask her Maker that one day, if it was His will, she might be able to walk again.

But one night she turned to her daughter Margaret, with a gentle smile. " I've been thinking," she said, " I'll not trouble the Lord any more about myself. If it is His will, I'll walk again. If not, I can be sure He has a purpose for me here."

Well, she never did walk again, but for the next three years she never lost her trust and when she fell asleep for the last time, it was with a smile and a prayer still on her lips . . .

TUESDAY—SEPTEMBER 23.

WORKING at the hedgeside as a roadman, Old Will has some odd things to say, but I'm not at all sure that he is half as daft as he sometimes likes to pretend. " A little bird told you," he insisted one day, " and I know fine how they do it. They sit up there on the telegraph wires, sucking the messages in wi' their feet ! "

Old Will wheels his bicycle along the highway every day, both to and from his work. Nobody has ever seen him ride it. " Don't you ever ride your bike ? " someone asked him. " No," he answered, " I just like to take it with me for the company ! "

THE FRIENDSHIP BOOK

THE trees, now decked in red and gold,
*   Their splendour soon will shed;*
But do not think, on winter days,
*   Their bare, black boughs are dead.*
Though autumn comes when few birds sing,
New life will stir again in spring !

THURSDAY—SEPTEMBER 25.

REALLY, I've no special reason for telling you this story, except that the Lady of the House loved it.

In every village, there's somebody like Mrs Miller. She's one of those friendly people, with never an ill word about a living soul, and a great favourite with the children. Added to that, Mrs Miller has the busiest pair of knitting needles in the village !

Every baby that's born there is sure to get a pair of boots or a jacket from Mrs Miller. Give her a few balls of wool and she'll run off a jumper in no time, and be glad to do it. But if ever her smile was the least bit wistful . . . well, perhaps it was because she'd no grandchildren of her own, and she always seemed to be knitting for others.

Then one day, great news ! Mrs Miller became a granny — not once, but twice over ! For at half-past nine in the morning her daughter gave birth to a boy—and at ten the same night, her son's wife had the prettiest little girl she's ever laid eyes on ! What a thrill it was for Mrs Miller.

Needless to say, her knitting needles are clicking away now faster than ever—and if a wee extra bit of love and care and pride go into every plain and every purl . . . well, if you're a granny yourself, you'll understand !

THE FRIENDSHIP BOOK

THE Lady of the House took a taxi to the station. " I'm rather late," she explained. (This is not unusual). " I'll get you there in time, Ma'am," said the driver; and he did !

I was waiting anxiously at the platform, with the tickets. As we settled in our corners while the train pulled out of the station, she told me about her experience. It was a particularly comfortable taxi, with a rug on the floor, tartan seat covers and everything spotless. She had offered a tip to the driver and he had refused, saying: " Not at all. This taxi is my own property, so I'm doing well enough."

Here was a man who gave just that little more in comfort and service, although he refused that little more in payment. And indeed isn't that what the whole world needs today; for us all to do just that little more than we are asked ?

SATURDAY—SEPTEMBER 27.

OUR family doctor, making out a prescription on the sitting-room table, paused for a moment. " I'm sure, Francis, that you have more sense than my last patient."

" How's that ?" I asked.

" Well, he looked at the bottle I produced and he said, ' I'm sure I'm not going to take a drop of that filthy-looking stuff.' "

" What did you tell him ?"

" I said, ' You can please yourself. It's not me that's going to cough !' "

We all use the words : " You've got to take your medicine." It's true. There comes a time when we must all face up to responsibility. But it's not often the words come home so clearly !

SUNDAY—SEPTEMBER 28.

BY their fruits ye shall know them.

MONDAY—SEPTEMBER 29.

ANNIE lived in a little house that had been her home ever since, as a bride, she had gone there nearly 60 years before.

Now she was alone, waiting peacefully for the end which she knew could not be far away. It was in those last weeks that she and her minister spoke of the slow hours of night when sleep is long in coming and when secret fears and anxieties tend to crowd the mind.

But Annie confessed that, even though she lay awake far into the night, she never worried. " What's your secret ?" asked the minister. " Do you count sheep until you fall asleep ?"

Annie smiled. " No," she nodded. " I don't count sheep. I talk to the Shepherd."

TUESDAY—SEPTEMBER 30.

IT was a lovely little bush in its brilliant autumn colouring. The Lady of the House, visiting the garden of a friend, examined it with delight. (For those with a gardening bent, it was a *Hypericum*, of the same family as the Rose of Sharon). " How perfect it is !" she exclaimed. " You don't often see this particularly graceful type. I used to have one like it, but it died." " But my dear," said her hostess, " it came from you. This one grew from a cutting which you once gave me. Don't you remember ?"

Soon the Lady of the House was on her way home with cuttings and now the pretty *Hypericum* grows in our garden again. Is it not a true saying: " What I gave, I have—what I kept, I lost " ?

OCTOBER

GOT some unpleasant task to do ?
Don't do it by and by.
Begin it now ! Don't put it off—
And here's the reason why:
You've got to do it ? Then, what fun
When you can say the task is done !

COME back over the years with me to the crew-room of an R.A.F. station in Lincolnshire in 1943.

There, in flying suits and helmets, a group of young airmen wait for the order that will send them into the night towards their target, for they are none other than the famous " Dambusters," Squadron 617.

Then, just before the order is given, one of their number takes out a Bible, opens it, and begins to read a passage to the others ... " If I ascend up into heaven, Thou art there; if I take the wings of the morning, even there shall Thy hand lead me; even the night shall be light about me ..."

Who was the man with the Bible ? He was Flight Lieutenant Jock Cook, D.F.C. His parents were in the Salvation Army, and young Jock had been raised in its great tradition. Oh, it would have been a temptation for a young man to hide his beliefs from the others, imagining they might scoff. But Jock did no such thing. And when his comrades discovered he was a Salvationist, far from scoffing, they asked him to say a few words before they took off on the mission from which they knew some might never return.

THE FRIENDSHIP BOOK

" TALK to me for five minutes," said a lively doctor the other day, " and I'll tell you what kind of man you are."

So I talked to him. And he kept his promise—though I decline to repeat what he said about me ! " How do you do it ?" I inquired.

He shrugged his shoulders and chuckled. " It's not intended to be taken too seriously," he said. " But there is something in it. As I go around I listen to what people say, and note the kind of things they like talking about. That tends to reveal the kind of mind and heart they have.

" It's a rough and ready method, I admit, but on the whole, men and women who like discussing ideas have what you might call great minds; folk who are liable to talk about events, especially unimportant events, have minds of average calibre." Then he paused. " And people," he added, " who are for ever discussing people, and finding fault with friends and neighbours, usually have small minds."

Perhaps there's a good deal in what he said.

AFTER the dinner, which was a wonderful meal, we helped our hostess to wash up—as is the way nowadays. We had been invited out for the evening by a professional woman, a spinster who, no doubt, has had her offers of marriage. Watching perhaps more than helping, one could not but notice this highly-paid woman's skill in the kitchen (which is certainly not supposed to be her sphere), her neatness, her accuracy, her love indeed of everything which goes to make a home. Probably every true woman is a homemaker at heart, first, last, and always !

THE FRIENDSHIP BOOK

SUNDAY—OCTOBER 5.

FREELY ye have received, freely give.

MONDAY—OCTOBER 6.

ONE Saturday I took a mother and father to an institution for mentally-retarded children.

I watched the parents being welcomed by their child, and when the visit was over, I saw them turn away, each with infinite heartbreak.

What can I say to those who make pilgrimages of this kind ? I extend to them my deepest sympathy and I can only add that it is surely true that carrying out such a duty must always be a little less grievous than leaving it undone.

TUESDAY—OCTOBER 7.

MARGARET inherited the china tea service, and kept it in her glass-fronted cabinet.

In the last forty years she has used the china only on very special occasions, but the other day it was in use because her youngest daughter, with her husband and two children, Peter and Eva, returned from America to settle in Scotland. So one or two old friends were invited, the best tea service was on the big mahogany table, and everybody talked at once.

Suddenly a piping voice silenced the chatter. " Granny," said wee Peter, " why is one of the cups different from all the others ?"

You could have heard a pin drop. At last Granny having looked at the cup, said slowly, " He's right ! All the pieces have ivy leaves except one, and that has clover leaves ! And to think, four generations have never spotted the clover leaf !"

Isn't it amazing what we miss ?

WEDNESDAY—OCTOBER 8.

*TROUBLE'S like a thistle that stands
        right in your way,
It cannot fail to grab you some sad or
        bitter day;
But why not walk around it as anyone
        can do ?
Never trouble trouble till trouble troubles
        you !*

THURSDAY—OCTOBER 9.

REV. O. LAIRD WHITE is chaplain to the deaf
    and dumb in the Highlands and Islands.

Before that he had a similar mission in St Helens,
Lancashire, and did everything he could to provide
a church for the deaf and dumb there. It meant
raising a great deal of money, and Mr White and
his helpers tried all the usual ways.

But Mr White believed in doing more. Somewhere he found an old barrel organ. Then every
Saturday afternoon he trundled it along to the
market place in St Helens and spent hours cheer-
fully turning the handle, while the grand old tunes
poured forth.

Even when the weather was wet and rough,
I'm told he stood his ground in the middle of
the busy market place, for every copper dropped
into his hat was a copper nearer the new chapel
he'd vowed to build.

It must have been an inspiring example to his
little flock to see their minister standing in the
rain, turning the barrel organ for all his worth—
and how splendidly his efforts bore fruit. Before
he left for Scotland, the deaf and dumb in St Helens
had their own church, where Sunday by Sunday
they gather to worship.

FRIDAY—OCTOBER 10.

LOVE is blind. Jim's aunts may ask each other what he sees in that girl he's taking round. It may be that Jim just cannot see her faults; and if that is so, then love does make lovers blind.

Or it could be that love opens the eyes, the inward eyes, so that those in love see, not less, but more than other people see—and the fact that so many young couples make a go of marriage, suggests that after all, as a rule, love is not blind.

Rabbi Julius Gordon once said—*Love is not blind. It sees more, not less. But because it sees more it is willing to see less.*

SATURDAY—OCTOBER 11.

PERHAPS it isn't surprising that Mrs Black had scarcely a good word to say about young folk.

Sixteen years ago her husband was beaten up by a teenage gang and spent many months in hospital. Then shortly after he got home there was an accident and he died.

As I say, it isn't surprising that Mrs Black's heart was filled with bitterness.

Then she learned of Stuart Grant, a young man who was giving up a job with excellent prospects to become an officer in the Salvation Army.

Mrs Black's whole attitude to young folk was changed by the good which Stuart did. On his days off he visited old folk, collecting prescriptions for them, bringing in coal, and doing jobs they couldn't do for themselves.

In fact, he has restored Mrs Black's faith in young folk after 16 bitter years.

As Stuart sets out on his new life, dedicated to others, may this tribute give strength to his right arm.

SUNDAY—OCTOBER 12.

HIM that cometh to Me I will in no wise cast out.

MONDAY—OCTOBER 13.

THE old " supply " minister stayed at the Guest House to take the pulpit for one Sunday only. By 11 a.m. there was no sign of him at the church. The duty elders gave him another five minutes. Then very reluctantly, the session clerk, who had never done it before, went into the pulpit to begin the service. Meantime, a younger and fleeter man was sent to the Guest House to investigate. " He was here at breakfast," said the landlady. " I thought he had gone off to the church." But they found him asleep in the drawing-room.

So it was about 11.30 a.m. before the session clerk was able to step out of the pulpit while the old man slipped by him on the way up. The rest of the service was conducted as if no upset had occurred. Only the choir may have noticed, as he came down again, that the minister was still wearing carpet slippers !

TUESDAY—OCTOBER 14.

TEN-SECOND sermons for a busy day.

If you can't make light of your troubles, keep them dark.

Difficulty, like the hill ahead, diminishes as you advance upon it.

It is magnificent to grow old if you keep young.

Happiness is the feeling you get when you're too busy to be miserable.

He who worries, doesn't trust. He who trusts doesn't worry.

THE FRIENDSHIP BOOK

YES, some folk bustle all day long—
Achieve an awful lot—
Yet have no time to hear about
The worries I have got.
God, slow me down that I can stay
To share somebody's grief today.

IF you happened to peep through a certain gate in Edinburgh, you might be surprised to see a group of men clad in overalls, peering into the open bonnet of a car.

But you'd be even more surprised to know they're not motor mechanics, but missionaries— and that the man in the dirtiest overall is a Glasgow minister, the Rev. Robert Bone.

You see, the job of a missionary today is in many ways different from what it was in the time of David Livingstone and Mary Slessor. Now, lorries and jeeps take the place of oxen and pack mules, and far greater distances can be covered. The trouble is that if a vehicle breaks down, it may be hundreds of miles to the nearest garage—so the missionaries must know how to do repairs.

That's why Mr Bone was called in. Not only was he a missionary in Africa for 15 years, but he also qualified as an engineer before he went out to the mission field. So, before the missionaries set out on their great work, he gives them a course of instruction which makes them ready for any emergency.

You know, I've usually found that the man who's not afraid to get his hands dirty does a grand job—and I'm sure Mr Bone and his merry men are no exception !

FRIDAY—OCTOBER 17.

ON his way back home from holiday, a friend of mine visited the R.A.F. Memorial at Runnymede.

There, high on a hill above the Thames, are the names of 10,000 airmen with no known grave— British, Canadian, South African, Rhodesian, Australian and many more who flew for freedom.

In a little alcove commemorating the airmen from Rhodesia stood a little vase of red and white carnations. It rested beneath the name of Pilot Officer Jack Money, who was killed in 1943, aged 20. A card on the flowers said—" From Mum and Dad."

Oh, yes, the Runnymede memorial is an impressive sight and a fitting tribute to brave men who never came back. But my friend tells me that, in some ways, that little vase of flowers with its poignant message from two proud, sad parents moved him more deeply than anything else.

SATURDAY—OCTOBER 18.

MR ANDREW BRAND recalls that as a boy some fifty years ago, he used to run errands for an elderly widow who could neither read nor write.

One morning she received a letter from her only son, in another town. He had sent her a pound note, and when Andrew came round that evening, she asked him to read the letter.

It said simply, " *Dear Mother, If you're all right, I'm all right.—Bobby.*"

Even yet, Andrew can see the tears glistening in the old lady's eyes, and the pride in her face.

I can't help thinking of all the lonely mothers throughout our land whose hearts would sing if only ten simple words like these came through their letter-box, telling them they are not forgotten.

THE FRIENDSHIP BOOK

IN the world ye shall have tribulation : but be of good cheer; I have overcome the world.

FOR a long time the children in Lennox Castle Hospital had been saving every scrap of silver paper they could lay their hands on. And when the parents came to visit their children, they brought some silver paper they'd saved as well. The children's target was to gather enough silver paper to pay for a guide dog for some blind person—no less than £250 worth.

Well, they succeeded at last. And when the folk at the guide dog centre heard of the special effort of the children, they took a lovely photograph of the dog, which they named Lennox, and sent it to the hospital, where it hangs in a place of honour.

No wonder Lennox looks so proud and happy ! For if he knows the story of how he came to be a guide dog (and the children are quite sure he does !) he couldn't be anything else but proud.

AFTER the baking was done the other night, the Lady of the House said to me: " Be a dear, Francis, and take some of these cakes round to Cousin Ruth. She hasn't been very well." Ruth was delighted with the little gift, saying as she accepted them: " Your wife did this ? Isn't she a clever kid !"

To her cousin, who is much older, my wife is still a child. It depends how you look on people and on things; maybe on how we look at ourselves. If we look on ourselves as old, or done, or useless, well, maybe we soon will be !

WEDNESDAY—OCTOBER 22.

A JOKE or a song or a handshake,
 A letter that comforts or cheers;
A meeting or parting, more precious
 Because of the smiles or the tears.
A five minutes' sit after dinner,
 A " Thank you " that lends the heart wings;
All these are but trifles, yet surely
 They're also life's wonderful things!

THURSDAY—OCTOBER 23.

MRS DOUGALL is a widow, and for many years Peter, her black cat, shared her home. You can imagine how much Peter's friendly presence helped the old lady, especially in the lonely days after her husband died.

Then there was an accident on the road, and the sad news was brought to Mrs Dougall that Peter had been run over and killed. Oh, what a heartbreak it was and how empty the house seemed that night.

But next morning there came a knock at the door. On the step stood a local farmer, who explained to Mrs Dougall that he heard she'd lost her cat. Then, reaching into his jacket, he drew out a wee, black ball of fluff and handed it to the old lady. Yes, it was a kitten, with blue eyes and pink nose— Peter's image in every way.

To say Mrs Dougall was thrilled is putting it mildly, and now Peter the Second is firmly in command of the household.

Maybe to most of us it's a little thing, but isn't it grand to think there are still folk left in this world who understand how something to care for, like this tiny black cat, can come between an old widow and utter loneliness?

THE FRIENDSHIP BOOK

HOSPITALS, some centuries ago, were far from being as we know them today. Only the poorest and most unfortunate would allow themselves be carried into hospitals, for their chance of recovery was probably much greater at home.

It so happened in the 17th century that a poor scholar once fell ill and was taken to hospital. Like all learned men at that time, he spoke Latin fluently. The doctors gathered round his bed, agreed that he seemed to have no friends and that he might therefore be a suitable subject for some medical or surgical experiment. Of course they spoke in Latin, thinking that the patient who lay so helpless in bed would not understand. But the sick man joined their conversation, asking in the same language: " Dare you call anyone worthless for whom Christ died ?"

Life is a precious gift to be cherished for all living beings — not only for ourselves.

A HOT land and a lady on holiday. Looking at a fine building she was unsure as to what it might be. Two little girls nearby indicated that she should come in with them. Then, lest the meaning be lost, each solemnly tied a handkerchief over her head. It was a church !

The older girl mounted the pulpit steps and commenced a sermon. " Amigos !" (friends), she said. It was a place for preaching ! The younger girl knelt at the front, clasping her hands and bowing her head. It was a place of prayer !

Language, to a little child, forms no barrier to friendship and communication. Would that we could keep their artless innocence right through our lives !

SUNDAY—OCTOBER 26.

FEED My lambs.

MONDAY—OCTOBER 27.

WHEN his father died young, Andy was given a job by an uncle who ran a small shop where he sold cloth by the yard. Jokingly, he told the 14-year-old Andy that they were in partnership together—and it was truer than Andy knew.

Never once did his uncle give him a lesson in salesmanship or explain the principles of buying or instruct him in book-keeping or preach a sermon on honesty. All the uncle did was to go about his business day by day, always punctual, pleasant to customers, shrewd in buying, watchful of expenses ... and inevitably Andy grew up to be like him. Later the small shop was his. He added other shops.

All of which reminds us that precept may be desirable but example is the thing !

TUESDAY—OCTOBER 28.

A FORMER Government scientist has been telling me how, during the war, it was his duty to work out certain statistics and then submit them to higher authority. His office or laboratory came to the conclusion that the average Englishwoman had 1.7 children and that she must live somewhere about the middle of the Bristol Channel !

This only shows how absurd scientists can become when they begin to treat human beings as no more than a set of figures. People are individuals, each with á heart, a mind, a soul, and each different to his or her neighbour. And it is surely this individuality that makes life full and interesting and worth living.

WEDNESDAY—OCTOBER 29.

LIFE'S grim for you ? Do not complain—
  Your face should hide your heart;
For others find the going hard:
  They, too, must play a part.
Your courage high, your spirit gay,
Meet trouble in a SPLENDID way !

THURSDAY—OCTOBER 30.

COMING down in the lift of a big store I overheard two men talking.

One said, " We couldn't think of it. We told her so."

" No," said the other, " it's not for her. It's a mansized job, if you ask me."

I should like to have asked what job was mansized. Instead I thought of those lines—

They talk about a woman's sphere
As though it had a limit.
There's not a place in earth or heaven,
There's not a task to mankind given,
There's not a blessing or a woe,
There's not a whispered " Yes " or " No,"
There's not a life or death or birth
That has a featherweight of worth,
Without a woman in it !

I might have recited these lines in the lift . . . but the two men got out on the first floor—dresses, silks, millinery, and evening gowns !

FRIDAY—OCTOBER 31.

SEEN on a wayside pulpit:—
  How good are you ? That is important.
What good are you ? That is important, too.
Searching questions, aren't they ?

NOVEMBER

A FEW years ago, Bob Hamilton was a business man in his early forties. He earned a good salary. He had few worries. Indeed, it was the kind of life many folk dream about. But for Bob it was not enough. It seemed to him he was living too much of his life for himself, and not enough of it for others.

So he decided to give up his job, and spend the rest of his life among the folk whom few seemed to care about—the down-and-outs, the homeless, alcoholics, drug addicts, the broken in spirit, and the friendless. It was no easy decision, for he is a married man with two sons to consider. But he went ahead with it, and today he is superintendent of the Mound Centre in Edinburgh, where all kinds of men come with every kind of problem.

Day after day he begins work at nine in the morning, and it is well after midnight until he returns home. Each day brings its difficulties. Sometimes there is discouragement—but never once since he took up his new life has he regretted it.

Oh, I have no doubt that if he had stayed where he was, he might have been making big money, and life would have been comfortable and secure. But, in helping lost souls to win their way back to the right road again, he has found rewards that cannot be measured.

To him, and all like him, I raise my hat solemnly and sincerely.

WHOSOEVER shall do the will of My Father which is in heaven, the same is My brother, and sister, and mother.

THE FRIENDSHIP BOOK

THE crime wave still rolls round the world. It causes infinite suffering and menaces life and property.

But I think we should never forget that however bad, nobody—no criminal—is wholly bad.

The late Sir Ben Turner reminds us of this. He once visited a Yorkshire prison specially to see a man sent there for stealing. The prisoner and Sir Ben shook hands; and the first words the prisoner uttered were—" How's my wife and the boy?"

We do well to consider ways and means of preventing crime, and it may be necessary to consider more severe penalties, but you and I ought never to forget that in the worst there is at least something of the best—a flicker of that flame of goodness which is in every man and woman.

EARLY in July a business man took a walk in his garden before going to the office. He snipped off some of his sweet-peas, took them with him when he drove into the city, and handed them to the office cleaner who, he happened to know, was finding life particularly hard at that time.

He had forgotten all about the incident until, one morning recently, the office cleaner, with apologies, handed him a small parcel wrapped in brown paper. Inside was a pair of bed socks. " Knitted them myself," murmured the cleaner. " Thought maybe with winter coming on they'd be nice for your mother."

And that is the end of the story, apart from the fact that I would like to make one comment. It is this kind of thing which enriches life and makes it, even in these cynical and often unkind days, very worthwhile.

WEDNESDAY—NOVEMBER 5.

THE richest man is he who finds
The best in each new day,
Who gathers harvests of bright things
And stores the good and gay.
In human dross he sees the gold—
He's rich and young though poor and old!

THURSDAY—NOVEMBER 6.

THE other night the Lady of the House and I spent the evening by the fireside, listening to the gramophone.

We played records of songs and music that, in their own way, have become unforgettable for us—the voices of today and of singers now gone; the music of great composers played by gifted musicians.

It was a grand evening and I told the Lady of the House about the man who made it all possible. He was born in a little town in Ohio, the son of an innkeeper. At 12 he became a newsboy on a train, and in the guard's van where he kept his newspapers he built a little laboratory where he experimented with his hobby, electricity.

One day, as he boarded a moving train with two armfuls of papers, he stumbled. It seemed for a moment he would fall beneath the wheels—but the guard caught him by the ears and pulled him to safety. It saved his life—but it was the start of a deafness that was to be with him all his days. Indeed, as an old man he wrote that he hadn't heard a bird sing since he was twelve—yet he went on to bring song and music to multitudes, for his name was Thomas Alva Edison, inventor of the gramophone.

Great blessings are often born of the sorest misfortunes, and the story of Edison surely proves it.

FRIDAY—NOVEMBER 7.

HAVE you heard this story of the boy who was in a sweet shop with his mother?

While she chatted with the woman behind the counter, the lad looked at one jar after another, pondering, pausing. "Oh, come on, Billy," exclaimed his mother at last.

"Just another minute," pleaded her son. "I've only a penny—so I've got to spend it carefully."

How right Billy was, to be sure. If you have a pound to spend, well, it matters little if you get a pennyworth of something you don't want. But if all the day's pleasure depends on what you buy with a penny, why, the possibilities are frightening.

I might add that you and I have only one life to spend; better be careful how we spend it, eh?

SATURDAY—NOVEMBER 8.

SOME time ago a Communist newspaper printed these words:—

"The gospel of Jesus Christ is a much more powerful weapon for the renewal of man and society than our Marxist philosophy is. For all that, we Communists will beat you Christians.

"We are a handful only. You Christians are numbered in millions. And we shall do it because we keep only what we need for living expenses out of our salaries or wages, and consecrate to propaganda all the rest of our money and all our free time and part of our holidays.

"You Christians, however, give only a very little time and money to the spreading of the gospel of Christ. How can anyone believe in your faith if you do not sacrifice money and time for it?"

My only comment on this is that, as a professing Christian, it made me think, and think hard.

SUNDAY—NOVEMBER 9.

THE wolf also shall dwell with the lamb, and the leopard shall lie down with the kid.

MONDAY—NOVEMBER 10.

IT seems that a radio station in British Columbia, Canada, runs a programme during which listeners are urged to telephone and give their opinions on any topic.

One Sunday, the subject for discussion was " God is Dead." The arguments raged heatedly for nearly an hour. Then a bolt of lightning knocked the station off the air for twelve hours !

The first phone caller, when the station came back on the air, said simply, " Galatians six, verse seven." This verse, you may remember, contains the words, " Be not deceived; God is not mocked."

TUESDAY—NOVEMBER 11.

ON Remembrance Sunday the folk of Paxton gather round their War Memorial, a stone cross standing at the crossroads. All are there—the Brownies and Cubs, the Scouts and Guides, old soldiers and mothers and widows. They share a short service and join in the National Anthem.

Then, one by one, the villagers move forward, take the scarlet poppies from their lapels, and thread them through the links of the chain surrounding the War Memorial until it seems ablaze with colour. Each one of them is paying his or her own tribute to the memory of the lads who marched away from their Border homes, never to return.

And when it is all over and the villagers have gone, and the War Memorial stands silent and deserted, the poppies remain, a unique salute to the fallen.

THE FRIENDSHIP BOOK

WHAT loneliness bereavement brings,
How strange each day to you.
Together there were happy things
Two loving hearts could do.
Gone are those years which made you glad;
Why not give thanks for joys you've had?

ON a spring day in 1851, a young couple in Aberdeen were blessed with their first baby, a boy. As they knelt by the crib, his mother whispered that her dearest wish was that one day he should be a missionary. Unhappily she was never to know if her dream would come true, for when Bobby was just a toddler of two she died.

But her husband knew how earnest her wish had been and he vowed that he would do everything he could to honour it.

Well, Bobby grew into a strapping lad. He became apprenticed to his father's trade of cabinet-maker, but when his day's work was over he went to night school and won a place at university.

It was a struggle, but young Bobby gained his M.A. degree, went on to qualify as a doctor, and at 24 was ordained as a medical missionary. It was the greatest day of his life when he sailed for Africa where he became the great Dr Robert Laws of Livingstonia. He founded more than 700 schools, laid the foundations of hospitals and colleges, and was honoured by king and country. Today, his memory is still beloved, and a fine new university will bear his name.

Surely that young mother's dream has come true in a far finer way than she could ever have imagined—and, indeed, it is still coming true.

FRIDAY—NOVEMBER 14.

MRS TURNER'S rheumatics were worse than ever. So much so that she mentioned to her daughter-in-law how badly the cold was affecting her.

Though she didn't know it, she was overheard by her little granddaughter. The wee girl didn't say anything at the time, but she so wanted to help her grandma. And apparently she decided there was only one thing to do.

That night she ended her prayers with these words —" And please, God, make it hot for Grandma."

It's so true, isn't it, that no matter how dark the way we've come or how uncertain the road ahead, laughter and love can never be far away when there's a little child near us !

SATURDAY—NOVEMBER 15.

UNLIKE other Anglican churches, Westminster Abbey comes under the authority of no bishop. It is known as " A Royal Peculiar." H.M. the Queen comes as official " visitor " from time to time, but otherwise the Dean and Chapter of Westminster Abbey are not subject to the same authorities as others.

" Peculiar " is a word with several meanings, of course. It can mean odd, strange, different, but it can also mean special, exceptional, particular, appropriate. When there is a good cause crying out for. support, or a wrong to be righted, all too often the people who give their support are labelled as " peculiar."

Many people are afraid of being thought "peculiar," through doing individual things, or speaking their minds freely. But what is first thought " peculiar " becomes right if just a few have the courage to support those who give the lead.

A WISH

Swimming, diving, all day long,
  If I could have a wish,
I'd leave the dry land far behind
  And change into a fish!

                              DAVID HOPE

HEALING

The hill and lake He took,
The murmur of a brook,
The sunset's burning glow,
The little winds that blow.

And then on all He laid
His peace in sun and shade,
That all with care enmeshed
Might find their souls refreshed.

DAVID HOPE

A HAVEN

You couldn't clock your hundred miles an hour,
This cobbled way is not what racers use;
But you've a chance instead to LIVE your hundred,
And as for me I know what I would choose.

DAVID HOP

THE FRIENDSHIP BOOK

SUNDAY—NOVEMBER 16.

REJOICE in the Lord alway : and again I say, Rejoice.

MONDAY—NOVEMBER 17.

THREE wee boys marched into the police station. Their heads barely reached the top of the counter but, by leaning forward, the duty sergeant could see they were holding two baby rabbits.

The boys had found the rabbits cowering by the fence at the side of the railway, close to the mother rabbit, which had been killed by the express. The boys decided the rabbits were too young to look after themselves, so they brought them to the police station, confident all would be well.

The sergeant scratched his head doubtfully. " Well, now, lads . . ." he began—and at that moment young Michael, who has just joined the police, stepped forward. " Leave it to me, sergeant," he said—and, taking the rabbits from the boys, he assured them he'd see they were well cared for.

Michael knocked up a hutch for them behind the police station. Before he goes on duty he sees they're fed and watered.

It's good to hear that, busy as policemen of today are, they're not too busy to care for two frightened little rabbits.

TUESDAY—NOVEMBER 18.

THESE sayings take only seconds to read, but they give thought enough for days.

He who does not live in some degree for others, hardly lives for himself.

He who has no faith in others shall find no faith in them.

THE FRIENDSHIP BOOK

WEDNESDAY—NOVEMBER 19.

SO many things I don't possess—
Alas, how poor am I;
And yet, so much of worth I have—
The hills, the trees, the sky;
The love of friends, my home, my health—
I simply cannot count my wealth!

THURSDAY—NOVEMBER 20.

SURELY one of the most moving moments during the funeral of Dr Martin Luther King came when a woman robed in white, a member of the choir in Dr King's own church, sang that beloved song, "If I Can Help Somebody," the words of which Dr King quoted in the last sermon he ever gave.

The words and music of the song came from an American woman who was born Alma Smith, 56 years ago in the town of Harriman, Tennessee, only 150 miles from Dr King's own birthplace.

Alma must have grown up to the haunting music of negro spirituals, and something in her own song echoes the greatest of them. She was just a young woman when she wrote it, and as she did so, I believe she was thinking of her mother's way of life. For when she completed it, she dedicated it to her mother.

I doubt if Alma ever realised that one day her song and its challenging message would reach out into all the world—and wherever she is now, she must have been proud to think her words were chosen to sum up the life of a great man—

If I can help somebody as I pass along,
If I can cheer somebody with a word or song,
If I can show somebody he is travelling wrong,
    Then my living shall not be in vain . . .

THE FRIENDSHIP BOOK

DURING the Korean war, an American General made a radio appeal for money to send urgently-needed medical supplies to the thousands of refugees made homeless by the war. Among those who listened to the broadcast was a little boy of eight—and as soon as it was finished, he left the house, trotted down to the chemist's on the corner, and bought a bottle of aspirins. Then, solemnly, he parcelled it up and sent it to the General.

That could have been the end of the story—but it wasn't. Somehow, the bottle of aspirins found its way straight to the General himself. He was a busy man, of course, but not too busy to read the boy's letter. When he did, he was so deeply moved that he made another broadcast simply to tell the whole land about it.

The end of the story is that, as a direct result of the little boy and his aspirins, a whole planeload of medical supplies was sent to Korea.

It's a parable, and its message is this—that however little you think you can do, do it now.

ARE you a bit stuffy?

I sometimes wonder what boys and girls must think of us, who are forty or fifty or sixty or more. What a chasm separates us from them. How differently we talk and think. How fixed in our ways we have become, how sure that we know everything and must always be right!

No wonder a boy once wrote in an essay—" The world is full of people who keep saying, ' *I was a boy myself once,*' but never show any signs of it."

Might we not unbend a little now and then, and practise being a bit younger?

SUNDAY—NOVEMBER 23.

JUDGE not, that ye be not judged.

MONDAY—NOVEMBER 24.

IT is 55 or so years since Captain Oates, one of Robert Falcon Scott's immortal heroes, went deliberately to his death. Knowing he was incurably ill and was a handicap to the little company trying so desperately to reach their depot in Antarctica, he said casually one morning—" I'm just going outside and may be some time." Then, without a good-bye, and in the most nonchalant manner, he crept out of the tent and walked into the blizzard—walked on and on till he fell, and his body was covered with snow.

It was a supremely brave act of sacrifice.

What made him do it? I am not quite sure. I suggest you think about it. Could it be that in each one of us there is something truly splendid—something more than knowledge or ability or understanding, something so urgent and so fine that it compels us to do things for others because we feel we must?

That very gallant gentleman died alone. I think he died happily.

TUESDAY—NOVEMBER 25.

I KNOW of no man who writes cheerier letters than Frank Reynolds.

This is from one of Frank's letters and I suspect it reflects much of what has been his own philosophy all his life:—

When up to your neck in trouble or boiling with indignation, remember the kettle. Though up to its neck in hot water, whenever it reaches boiling point it begins to sing!

THE FRIENDSHIP BOOK

WEDNESDAY—NOVEMBER 26.

NOBODY knows what a prayer can do
When somebody, somewhere, prays for you . . .
Clearing a path through the tangled track,
Easing the strain on the breaking back.
When hope fades away and is lost to view—
Nobody knows what a prayer will do.

THURSDAY—NOVEMBER 27.

FOR years a friend of mine has been a blood donor.
Every once in a while he has reported to the centre, given a pint of blood, had a rest and a cup of tea—and, as far as he was concerned, that was the end of it until the next call came.

But recently he was asked if he could come to the Infirmary one Thursday morning. " You see," the nurse explained, " a little girl with the same blood group as you is going through a hole-in-the-heart operation. We'll need you to help her."

Of course, my friend was there. Nothing would have kept him away. It was the first time in his years as a blood donor that he had ever learned whom he was helping.

Oh, he never doubted that his blood meant life for someone. But somehow, knowing that what he was doing was helping a child in the most critical hour of her life . . . that, in a way, her whole future depended on him as well as on the surgeons and nurses . . .why, that made all the difference in the world.

Indeed, he found himself thinking of her and praying for her.

I don't expect he will ever know the girl's name. But I can say this—when he makes his next visit to the transfusion centre, he will go with a new understanding of the part he is there to play.

FRIDAY—NOVEMBER 28.

THIS is term day throughout Scotland. It may pass without much notice, but time was when it had to be the occasion for thousands to move from one home to another. A friend recalls "The Buggy Van" just before the war, whose staff, for a statutory fee of 2s 6d, sprayed all the furniture with insecticide before removal from an old property to a new one; regardless of the fact that such treatment was not always needed.

Shifted to a council house in 1938, our friend remembers how her mother was heartbroken at having to remove for the great distance of three miles! But they had fun in those days, too, and laughter. Purses held less, and although joys were perhaps simpler, they were none the worse for that.

SATURDAY—NOVEMBER 29.

IN her younger days, Mrs Hunt, of Pietermaritzburg, kept a book in which she wrote down every saying and quotation that appealed to her.

Some she read in books. Some she heard in the passing. All are, in their way, pearls of their kind. And now, in the evening of her days, Mrs Hunt turns the pages of her book, and finds comfort in the thoughts of long ago.

From her home in South Africa, she passed on several to me, and I have chosen one which, though anonymous, puts in a nutshell much of what I have always tried to say:—

When I dig a man out of trouble, the hole that is left is the grave in which I bury my own trouble.

SUNDAY—NOVEMBER 30.

WE walk by faith, not by sight.

DECEMBER

A MINISTER friend said, "Here's a question that many people have asked me. It's—'Why does a minister wear a gown in the pulpit?'"

"Perhaps it has something to do with the robes worn by the disciples," I ventured. "Or is it connected in some way with the Reformation?"

My friend smiled. "No, Francis," he replied. "It's to keep the minister warm!"

It seems that in the old days churches were unheated and draughty. So the ministers took to wearing long robes to keep the cold out.

Yes, it's as simple as that! But I feel that many of us often make the same mistake—of trying to find a complicated solution to a problem, when all the time the simple answer is right under our nose.

CANON ELLIOTT looked at a steeplejack walking a plank 180 feet above the pavement. It made him dizzy to watch. When the steeplejack came down, the canon said—"However do you do it? I could no more do that than fly."

"Go on with you," retorted the steeplejack with a grin. "Of course you could. Look, there's a plank lying in the grass. Walk on it! See . . . you can walk on it when it's on the ground, so you can walk on it when it's in the sky. Same plank. Same width. Just get on with your job and don't look down! You're as right as rain, guv'nor!"

The steeplejack was right, of course! It's the *not* looking down that takes such a lot of doing. Looking up is always safer—and better!

WEDNESDAY—DECEMBER 3.

WHEN people are unkind to you,
  It makes things ten times worse
If you hit back or sulk or fret,
  Or weep a lot or curse.
But if you're big enough to grin,
Why, strangely, you're the one to win!

THURSDAY—DECEMBER 4.

GLANCING through a Scout's diary the other day, I found these thoughts:—

A Scout is always trustworthy. A Scout is always loyal. A Scout is always helpful. A Scout is always friendly. A Scout is always courteous. A Scout is always kind. A Scout is always cheerful. A Scout is always thrifty. A Scout is always brave. A Scout is always reverent.

Well, I'm not a Scout and neither, perhaps, are you—but that's no reason why we shouldn't all bear these ideals in mind.

FRIDAY—DECEMBER 5.

ALEXANDER DUNCAN, who is just over 80, came out of hospital recently, completely recovered after a serious illness.

" I've just taken my driving test again," he told me the other day. " I wanted to be sure that I was still fit to drive—at my age. They let me pass, too, with flying colours !" Then after a moment's pause he added, " What's more, I've just ordered a new car and a new suit."

Well, Alexander, you may be far past the Psalmist's three score years and ten, but you still display an attitude of responsibility which does you credit.

THE FRIENDSHIP BOOK

THERE is a story of a Cambridge don who, some years ago, was admired or reviled for his simple delight in his concertina. Brilliant as he was, he liked nothing better than picking up his very small musical instrument, bought at a junk shop, and playing anything he had heard.

One of his students surprised him when he was playing. The student, a rich American, listened fascinated. " Say," he said eagerly, " I'd like to play like that. If I get an instrument, will you teach me?"

Off went the American, returning in no time with the most fabulous accordion you can imagine.

So the don did his stuff, and the American learned slowly, till at last he said—" Say, I don't seem to get the hang of this clumsy instrument somehow. I'll swap you mine for yours!"

Seems to me there's a lesson in this somewhere!

GOD loveth a cheerful giver.

A SCHOOL teacher asked her class during a lesson, " How many of you would like to go to heaven?"

The whole class held up their hands—except one wee lass. She sat solemnly with her head bowed.

Then, just as the teacher was about to ask why she didn't want to go to heaven, the boy next to the girl nudged her and said—

" Put up your hand, Jean. She doesn't mean right now!"

TUESDAY—DECEMBER 9.

MANY fine stories have been told about Sir Harry Lauder, but this one seems to me to sum up all that he was and what he stood for.

It happened one Sunday night during the war. Officially, of course, Sir Harry had retired, but he was always ready to help a good cause, and that night he was appearing at the King's Theatre, Glasgow, on behalf of the Red Cross.

It was a great moment when the stocky figure marched to the centre of the stage, to the cheers of the audience. Some of them at once began to call for songs he had made his own—" Roamin' In The Gloamin'," " I Love A Lassie," and many more.

Sir Harry held up his hand for silence. A hush fell over the crowded theatre. Quietly he said, " Ladies and gentlemen, this is the Sabbath." So, instead of singing one of his favourites, he sang in his rich, strong voice that old song of faith and trust, " Rocked In The Cradle Of The Deep."

> Secure I rest upon the wave,
> For Thou, O Lord, hast power to save,
> And calm and peaceful is my sleep,
> Rocked in the cradle of the deep . . .

I am not one of those killjoys who want to return to the days when to smile on Sunday was a sin. But if we all had something of Sir Harry's pride in the Sabbath, wouldn't life be that bit finer?

WEDNESDAY—DECEMBER 10.

> **W**HEN *coughs and colds are everywhere,*
> *When snow is on the ground,*
> *When ills and chills make living grim*
> *When money won't go round,*
> *Not while the blossom's on the bough*
> *Need we to wear a smile, BUT NOW!*

THURSDAY—DECEMBER 11.

IN the nursery school the tiny tots were rehearsing the Nativity Play. Jean Robertson, the nurse in charge, was putting the little players through the motions and the few words that each had to speak. Suddenly the door flew open. In whirled another tiny figure, black masked and wearing a black cloak. "WHAM! BANG! BONK!" he cried, his small arms revolving in all directions. "What on earth is this?" demanded Jean of the minute figure in black. He could not have been more than five years old—at the very most. "It's Batman versus Mary and Joseph!" he explained.

His words were truer than he knew. In every generation the noisy, the vulgar, and the destructive fight a constant battle against the old, the beautiful, and what has been held sacred for countless generations.

FRIDAY—DECEMBER 12.

EVER heard this story of a stoker aboard a tramp steamer?

His was a hard job—hot, backaching work, for his boilers needed constant attention.

A hum-drum existence, if you like . . . but he was the cheeriest of men. He shovelled dusty coal into blazing furnaces with sweat and song, and in sunshine or storm, north or south of the equator, you could hear him chanting—

There's gotta be a glory in the work you do,
A Hallelujah chorus in the heart of you;
Paint or tell a story, sing or shovel coal,
There's gotta be a glory or the work lacks soul!

And there's only one person who can put a glory into the routine jobs you have to do, and that's *you*.

SATURDAY—DECEMBER 13.

MISS MARGARET tells me that one day not long ago, she went to a friend's house for a cup of tea and a chat. On the mantelshelf was a tiny framed notice.

" It struck me at once," Miss Margaret tells me. " And I had to smile. My hostess loves nothing better than having folk in for a natter, but she is a shrewd body, and knows very well that talk can be dangerous—hence the card with its blunt truism for all to read and inwardly digest—
A slip of the foot may soon be recovered, but that of the tongue perhaps never.

" My hostess never referred to the notice on the mantelshelf, and the two of us talked fifty to the dozen . . . but I was always mindful of the warning."

SUNDAY—DECEMBER 14.

BE not forgetful to entertain strangers : for thereby some have entertained angels unawares.

MONDAY—DECEMBER 15.

IF the going is hard for you, I want to say :
I have known the rough, steep places along the road of life. I have known what it is to come perilously near to despair. I have lost faith in God and man—and in my own ability to ride out the storm.

Like you, of course, I have hidden behind a facade, smiling, cracking a joke, swinging along, but like you I have come face to face with grim realities when alone, when groping in the dark. It is a terrible thing to feel lost and helpless.

And there's only one answer. Keep plodding on from day to day, and somehow you will find the load is lighter and the way ahead clearer.

THE FRIENDSHIP BOOK

ONE cold evening during Christmas week, a lonely old man sat sadly by the fire in his home. He was the Rev. William McDermott, who, in more than 40 years' ministering to the people of Glasgow, wore himself out. His health broke down, he had a stroke, and now he can move around only with a stick.

Through all his trouble, his one great comfort was his wife—but a few months before Christmas she died. Friends, of course, keep in touch, and the neighbours are kindness itself. Even so, Mr McDermott couldn't help thinking what Christmas would be like without his wife at his side.

That's when there was a knock at the door. On the step were four young men students, their scarves round their necks, and their faces aglow. They greeted Mr McDermott cheerfully and gave him a box of groceries they'd brought as a Christmas gift. Then they announced they'd also clean the windows, bring in coal—indeed, anything the old minister might have difficulty in doing himself.

It wasn't long before the four smiling cavaliers were off again—to surprise some other old and lonely soul—leaving Mr McDermott with a full heart. He felt the visit was, in a way, a sermon specially for him—not preached, but lived by the four students.

THE gifts you get at Christmas
May thrill you to the core;
I hope they shower on you
In lots, and then some more!
But if you really want to live,
The secret is to give and give!

THURSDAY—DECEMBER 18.

IN the autumn of 1741, an old man shuffled aimlessly back to his lodgings in London.

An illness a year or two before had left him partly paralysed. Now it seemed there was little left for him in life. As he entered his room, he caught sight of an envelope which had lain on his desk, unopened, for days. Idly he picked it up and drew a manuscript from it, with a letter asking him to set the words to music.

For a moment the old man almost tossed it aside—but something in the words stirred his heart. Spellbound, he sat down and began to write.

For 24 days he hardly left his desk. But, in those 24 days, the world had been given what is perhaps the musical masterpiece of all time—for the old man was Handel and the music his " Messiah."

FRIDAY—DECEMBER 19.

IN one of her books, Elizabeth Byrd tells how she spent a stormy winter night in a cottage on a bleak slope among lonely hills in Scotland. When the wind howled and the rain poured from a black sky there came a knock at the door, and a neighbour's thin, undergrown, crippled boy came limping in. He had been sent by his mother to ask if Mrs MacIntosh was all right, and was surprised to find she had a visitor.

As an exceptionally fierce gust shook the shutters, the lad looked curiously at Elizabeth Byrd and asked if she were frightened.

" Of course she was scared before you came," replied Mrs MacIntosh instantly. " But now we've a man about !"

Some folk have the gift for saying things that make a cripple feel strong, a child feel important.

SATURDAY—DECEMBER 20.

I FOUND this verse on a Christmas card. It's worth thinking about.

He prayed for strength that he might achieve,
He was made weak that he might obey.
He prayed for health that he might do great things,
He was given infirmity that he might do better things.
He prayed for riches that he might be happy,
He was given poverty that he might be wise . . .
His prayer was answered—he was most blessed.

SUNDAY—DECEMBER 21.

GLORY to God in the highest, and on earth peace, good will toward men.

MONDAY—DECEMBER 22.

IN Britain, this is the shortest day. As the street lamps are lit so early, I find myself thinking about one or two lines from Robert Louis Stevenson.

My tea is nearly ready and the sun has left the sky;
It's time to take the window and see Leerie going by;
For every night at tea-time and before you take your seat,
With lantern and with ladder he comes posting up the street.

Well the lamplighter, like so much more, has gone. But perhaps we should all take a moment or two out of our day-to-day lives to stop and look up at the stars above us and wonder at the infinite beauty created by God. Surely He is the Lamplighter who has given us the greatest comfort in our darkness.

TUESDAY—DECEMBER 23.

THE Lady of the House and I agree that one of our most unforgettable Christmas memories is of an evening service in a little church we visited years ago.

During the day snow had fallen, and now the sky was a myriad of twinkling stars. Inside, the church was warm and cosy, and in darkness save for the lights of the Christmas tree in the corner.

During the service, a little lad of ten stepped forward, and in a pure treble voice sang that lovely Christmas hymn, " Once In Royal David's City."

Every time I hear it, I picture him again—but I also remember another lad who was brought up in a country vicarage in Buckinghamshire. His name was Henry Gauntlett, and he, too, loved music and singing. At nine he was organist of his father's church. But his father wanted him to become a lawyer—and he did. Then at forty, after his father died, he gave up the law for music.

He became the most distinguished organist of his time, and it was he who wrote the tune which has made " Once In Royal David's City " beloved throughout the world:—

He came down to earth from heaven
    Who is God and Lord of all.
And His shelter was a stable,
    And His cradle was a stall.

WEDNESDAY—DECEMBER 24.

THE shepherds, upward looking, saw
    A shining star above;
The shepherds, with humility,
    Looked down on perfect love.
May Christmas, ere its touch be gone,
Teach me that light and love are one!

THURSDAY—DECEMBER 25.

THERE is a legend of a boy named Melchor, who lived in a far country and was told by an angel of the birth of Christ. Filled with a longing to see and worship the Holy Child, Melchor set off on a pilgrimage to Bethlehem, but the road was long and hard. He had mountains to cross and rivers to ford. Often he was lost. More often he was hungry; and it was three years before he at last traced the Holy Child, finding him playing in the dust of the street.

Told that this was indeed the King of Kings, he bowed to the ground; and as he did so, the child Jesus climbed on his back, and Melchor for a time became His donkey, carrying Christ.

Melchor then set off for his home, and the road ran between grass and flowers. He had singing birds for company, and found himself at his journey's end in a single day.

Does this ancient Christmas legend not remind us that the good things in life are worth striving for?

FRIDAY—DECEMBER 26.

"DADDY," said the little boy, "I do like Grandma, don't you?"

"Of course, I do," smiled his father. "She's my mother."

The boy thought for a moment, his brow furrowed. "Oh," he murmured, "I didn't know that." Then he added, "But when I grow up I'm going to marry Gran, I like her so much."

His father smiled again. "Son," he protested gently, "you can't marry my mother, surely?"

Again the wee boy frowned, but like magic his face cleared. "Why not?" he asked triumphantly. "You married my mother, didn't you?"

SATURDAY—DECEMBER 27.

DID you hear about the housewife who went out specially to buy two pounds of sugar because she had run out of it? She was vexed that she had made such a silly mistake.

The minute she had filled the sugar basin she stood on a stool to put the bag on a shelf in her kitchen cupboard, moved a tin to the right . . . and there, plain as plain, was a two-pound bag of sugar.

She was mad. She called herself names. She had made an unnecessary journey.

And then she chuckled. After all, why should she grumble? She was better off than she had realised.

We often are.

SUNDAY—DECEMBER 28.

PEACE to him that is far off, and to him that is near.

MONDAY—DECEMBER 29.

SOON we'll all be wishing one another a Happy New Year.

But this story is about a man for whom the years, old and new, had been anything but happy. Indeed, life held so little for him that he made up his mind to end it all by jumping from a bridge into a river which flowed through the city.

He started out on his last, lonely walk—and as he strode on, he said to himself—" If I meet just one happy-looking person before I get there, I will change my mind and go on living."

That is the end of the story—but the question that remains for every one of us is simply this— *Suppose that man had met me or you . . . would he have turned back or walked on ?*

TUESDAY—DECEMBER 30.

DARK days there'll be for you and me—
No doubt we'll grouse awhile;
But courage and a bit of faith
Will help us all to smile.
Be strong, let not your spirits fear—
There's lots of joy to come next year!

WEDNESDAY—DECEMBER 31.

" HEAVENLY Father, Thou hast brought us safely to the present day."

No hymn, surely, could be more appropriate for the last day of the year. But I wonder how many realise that, in a way, it was pure chance that it ever came to be written—and its writer never really intended it for our hymn books at all.

She was a Bedfordshire girl, Hester Hawkins, who had an ideally happy home and a deep and abiding love for her father and mother. As they grew older, and approached their golden wedding anniversary, Hester decided to give them a very special gift—something they could share, and carry with them on the last miles of their road together.

Yes, it was the very hymn we sang last week. It touches on the shadows and sunshine of their long life together, of their moments of doubt, of their sorrow at the death of one of their children

If you read it over again, you will see how fitting a gift it made for the old couple:—

Yet Thy love hath never left us
    In our griefs alone to be,
And the help each gave the other
    Was the strength that came from Thee.

I like to think it will be our prayer, just as it was theirs.

A Happy New Year to you all.

Where the Photographs were taken

HOLIDAYS — *Edinburgh.*

SERVICE — *Nunraw, East Lothian.*

THE WAY OF THE GEESE — *Aberlady Bay, East Lothian.*

THE UNSEEN GIFT — *Chichester Cathedral, Sussex.*

A DAY TO REMEMBER — *Rescobie Loch, Angus.*

POTATO TIME — *Barry, Angus.*

BEHIND THE DREAM — *Stourhead, Wiltshire.*

ANYTHING FOR ME? — *New Mill, Penzance, Cornwall.*

TIME — *Knowle, Warwickshire.*

OUT OF THE SHADOWS — *On Beinn an Lochain, Argyll.*

WORKING TOGETHER — *Kyle of Durness, Sutherland.*

THE HEART OF THINGS — *Meriden Cross, Warwickshire.*

ALL AS ONE — *Alyth, Perthshire.*

GUESSING — *Ashdown Forest, Sussex.*

LEARNING — *Dovedale, Derbyshire.*

FIRST STEPS — *St Giles Cathedral, Edinburgh.*

GOOD NEIGHBOURS — *Dundee, Angus.*

THE INTRUDER — *Loch Leven, Argyll.*

LEGS BEFORE WHEELS — *St Andrews, Fife,*

THE ABBEY STEPS — *Fountains Abbey, Yorkshire.*

SEA MUSIC — *Portpatrick, Wigtownshire.*

BEGINNINGS — *Falls of Dochart, Killin, Perthshire.*

PATIENCE — *King's Mill, Shipley, Sussex.*

HEALING — *Derwent Water, Keswick, Cumberland.*

A HAVEN — *Lewes, Sussex.*

Printed and Published by D. C. THOMSON & CO., LTD.
12 Fetter Lane, Fleet Street, London, E.C.4.
© D. C. Thomson & Co., Ltd., 1968.